STATISTICAL ASSESSMENT OF RECORDS MANAGEMENT SYSTEM IN SIERRA LEONE

PRINCE SAO LAHAI, JR.

*(Librarian at Department of Library,
Fourah Bay College,
University of Sierra Leone)*

Published by
*TalNet Independent Publishers
Harare Zimbabwe*

Copyright: 2020 by Prince Sao Lahai Jnr

All right reserved: No part of this book may be reproduced in any form, by Photostat, microfilm, retrieval system, or any other means, without prior written permission of the publisher.

TalNet Independent Publishers
Harare, Zimbabwe
+263778312138
talnetpublishers@gmail.com

ISBN: 9781928533986

Cover Design: TalNet Independent Publishers
Printed in Zimbabwe
Printed by TalNet Printers

Table of Contents

PREFACE 5
FOREWORD 8
INTRODUCTION 9
PART 1: 14
THEORETICAL CONCEPT OF RECORDS MANAGEMENT AND ARCHIVES ADMINISTRATION 14
    Introduction 14
    Development of Records Management 14
    Policies, Procedures and Guidelines 16
    Records and Archive Management Profession 17
    Freedom of Information and Records Management 21
    Principles and Practices of Records Management 24
    Reformation of records Management Programme 28

PART 2: 32
THE MANAGEMENT OF PUBLIC SECTOR FINANCIAL RECORDS 32
    Introduction 32
    Financial Records Management Policy 32
    Financial Information/Records 34
    Financial Records Management and Accountability 37
    Monitoring and Compliance 40
    Financial Management and Records Management 44
    Financial Records Keeping and Information Technology (IT) 47
    Competency and Experience in Managing Records 48

PART 3: 52
THE MANAGEMENT OF ELECTRONIC RECORDS 52
    Introduction 52
    Definitions and Types of Electronic Records 52

    Challenges of Managing Electronic Records 54

    Regulatory Framework of Electronic Records Management 56

    Guidelines, Policies, Procedures for Electronic Records 60

    IT Specialist and Records Manager..66

    Importance of Keeping Electronic Records...69

PART 4: 73

SURVEY APPROACH TO RECORDS MANAGEMENT 73

    Introduction 73

    Research Variables 73

    Population studied 74

    Research sample 74

    Research Instrument 76

    Method of Collecting Data 78

    Method of Analysing Data 79

    Ethical Considerations..81

    Constraints 83

PART 5: 84

ANALYSIS AND DISCUSSION 84

    Introduction 84

    Specific Objectives 85

    Z-Score and Probability Value Test for the Variables................................124

PART 6: 127

SUMMARY, CONCLUSIONS AND OBSERVATIONS......................................127

    1. INTRODUCTION 127

    2. SUMMARY...127

    3. CONCLUSIONS 129

    4. OBSERVATIONS 139

BIBLIOGRAPHY 143

PREFACE

The management of public sector records over the years in Sierra Leone has nothing to talk home about. This is evident in the low Gross Domestic Product (GDP) of the country of less than 7.5%. The reason for this minimal figure can be partly attributed to the mismanagement of resources (human and materials) which are not accounted for through supporting records for the overall development of the country. Thus the lack of transparency and accountability through records has often been the chronic records management problems which affect every Ministries, Departments and Agency (MDAs). These chronic records management problems have been the contributing factors for the suffering of a vast majority of Sierra Leoneans which cast the blame squarely on bad governance. This situation has been manifested in the political dispensation of past and present governments over the control of scarce resources (human and materials) for the overall development of the country. Thus for good governance, transparency and accountability to exist in any organisation there must be good records management system.

This book is the product of the researcher's thesis which investigated the effective management of records at Ministry of Finance and Economic Development (MoFED), Sierra Leone in relation to good governance, accountability and transparency. This book is a multi-purpose book for every library, Archive and information studies students, Ministry, Department, and Agencies (MDAs) that may like to know the status of records management system in Sierra Leone; Researchers whether within or liberal Art or the other disciplines that may like to know the procedure of using descriptive statistics to analyse research data, using statistical formula to test hypotheses like the Z-score methods in this book. The objectives of the study were to: identify the types of records generated and received by MoFED; identify the records structures, procedures and regulatory requirements governing their keeping; investigate whether or not the management of records at MoFED is consistent with the life cycle concept of records keeping; investigate staff training and competency in records keeping at MoFED; investigate the challenges staff and users face in managing and using records at MoFED; explore the relationship between the MoFED registry/administration and the National Archives among others.

This study was a survey approach which employed questionnaire, interview, observation and documentary analysis as methods to collect data. The sample of the study was randomly selected from key Civil Servant Officers (CSO), Contract Officers (CO) and other staff at the MoFED registry/administration unit. Sixty (60) participants were selected of which fifty (50) fully participated in the study. Data were analysed using Statistical Package for the Social Sciences (SPSS, Version 16) to compute frequencies, percentages and extrapolate pie and bar charts. SPSS was also used to compute Z-score and Probability value to test variables against the stipulated probability level of significance at five percent (5%).

The findings of this study revealed that there is decentralised management of records at MoFED in general but MoFED registry/administration in particular is devoid of holding financial records. The findings also revealed that MoFED has laws and policies for the management of records but these policies are neither enforced nor effectively utilised to solve records management problems. The findings further revealed that there is inadequate trained and qualified middle level staff for managing records. The findings discovered inadequate facilities, equipment and supplies at MoFED registry/administration in preserving records. The findings further revealed that electronic records management exists but there are no formal electronic management policies especially with retention and disposition procedures. Also, there is a relationship between MoFED and the National Archives but not quite strong. Finally, the findings revealed that ten (10) or seventy-one percent (71%) of the variables passed the test to support the hypothesis of the study.

The study concludes that MoFED should employ more trained and qualified middle level staff for the management of both paper and electronic records in order to enhance good governance, accountability and transparency. MoFED should also provide more facilities, equipment and supplies and MoFED registry/administration should also hold financial records.

FOREWORD

As the management of records in organisations is very pivotal, be they private or public sector; it is imperative for every organisation to embark on good records management practices and procedures. Organisations have been facing difficulties to manage their records in such a way that will enhance their ultimate goals. This book then is in the right direction for that purpose; it is intended to attain organisations goals and eliminate weaknesses and concentrate on their strengths.

This book clearly used the statistical tools in analysing data collected from the field, especially the use of Z-score value to test the variables used in justifying the alternative hypothesis as against the null hypothesis to show users of records that when records are managed effectively and efficiently in organisations it could enhance transparency, accountability for records especially financial record management.

Associate Prof. John Abdul Kargbo

Dean, Faculty of Arts, Fourah Bay College, USL

INTRODUCTION

Sierra Leone lies on the West coast of Africa 28,000 square miles (72,000km^2) in area and bordered on the West by Guinea and Liberia with a population of seven million and ninety-two thousand one hundred and thirteen (7,092,113). It has a great diversity in the area of natural components that comprise varied topography, climatic condition as well as vegetation patterns. Sierra Leone has a Gross Domestic Product (GDP) of less than 7.5%, with a low per capita income of citizens. The rationale for this appalling figure of GDP can be partly attributed to the mismanagement of resources (human and materials) which are not accounted for via supporting records for the overall development of the country. Thus, the lack of transparency and accountability through records has often been the chronic records management problems which affect every Ministries, Departments and Agency (MDAs). These chronic records management problems have been the contributing factors for the suffering of a vast majority of Sierra Leoneans which cast the blame squarely on bad governance. This situation has been manifested in the political dispensation of past and present governments over the control of scarce resources (human and materials) for the overall development of the country. As good governance issues become immensely important, records keeping should be attentively paid to. This is evidenced in people's rights and responsibilities as records have unlimited primary value. On this note, it could be realised that any nation which cannot highly regard record keeping hardly develops without the existence of good information. This is because information has been considered a commodity essential to planning for national development in such a nation.

Records are regarded as information, in any format, detailing the transaction of business whether profit or non-profit making organisations. Records include all books, papers, maps, photographs, machines readable materials and other documentary materials regardless from physical form or characteristics, made or received by individuals in the transaction of public business and preserved by the managers or its legitimate successors as evidence of individual organisations' functions, policies, decisions, procedures, operation or other activities of the organisation. Thus the keeping of records and storage of information in an organisation has become critical not only for historical purposes but also, and more importantly for current and future managerial and policy development. Records have been used as tools and instruments to understand organisations and to use them as a basis for improvement, comparison with other agencies and secure resources.

Record is defined also as information which provides legal evidence. It can be verified; its context can be demonstrated and it can be shown that it has been protected from corruption. Another definition of record is a document in any form or medium created, received, maintained and used by an organisation or an individual in pursuance of a legal obligation or in the transaction of business. For records management is defined as both a discipline and management function concerned with the sustainable application of management techniques to and control of the information created or received in normal information of an organisational business. Unlike many information sources, records have a more distinct cycle that includes creation, processing, distribution, maintenance, evaluation, and ultimate disposition (i.e either destruction or transmittal for permanent housing in an archive, vault, or other dedicated facility operated by the organisation). Records management is the manner in which official records such as correspondence and files with information organised in such a way that they can have a meaning and be used continuously by users such as ministers, managers, records professionals, educational institutions, legal authorities, the donor community and any other interested parties.

Records management in Sierra Leone is increasingly becoming an important instrument which determines the management of change process upon which modern management principles and practices depend. The Public Sector Reform (PSR), for example, taking place in Sierra Leone depends on records and information that have been logically organised and stored, thus giving meaning to users. They are instruments toward the past as well as forecasting and planning for the future. Records management has not only become an instrument for good management but has developed into a recognised discipline and field of study, both in educational institutions as well as government departments. It has, therefore, become an international instrument and message which can be given the same meaning. And it can be shared between and amongst users in different parts of the world. Thus the development of technology has also had an impact on the way records are kept and information stored. Many records in organisations are now digitised making it necessary for users to be computer- proficient in order to interpret the information accurately.

'Good Governance' on the other hand can be described as a basis for sustainable development. Good governance is borrowed from the corporate entity dating back from the Global Consulting Firm at Mckinsey and Co.'s surveys of institutional investors around the world to determine the importance of the governance process to a progressive economy. It is the process by which managers organise themselves, function, exercise authority and ensure continuity. In the context of the public sector, good governance can be viewed as the process by which power, authority and influence are defined and achieve desired public policy objectives in political, economic, social and other sectors. In the political sector there is evidenced that the role of the state has been redefined to meet the new demands by citizens for transparency and accountability. In this case the movement towards greater democracy, culminating into open and just government, has depended on organised and well-managed information systems and records. The promotion of good governance and accountability could not have been successful without available and accessible records and information which citizens can use as a basis for their demands. Governments that have tried to suppress information have been frustrated by the spread of information in their countries from the international community. It is possible for citizens to see whether or not the government is transparent and accountable via the availability of records which can be used as evidence in policy making. Thus well-managed records and information systems are important instruments for gauging transparency via the formulation of standards of conduct for public officials.

In the economic sector, the re-classification of roles has been made by some governments of the state through for example concentrating on the areas they can best manage and leave other responsibilities to private sectors, public enterprises and non-governmental organisations. The state in the demarcation of powers, for example, would be responsible for creating a conducive environment for investment. In doing so it must provide information about its governance, democracy, and protection of its citizens, rule of law, and above all, its management of resources and revenue which includes fiscal and monetary policies. In that direction records management has become a critically important instrument not only in managing but also in reforming the public sector and the civil service machinery of government. For any reform to take place there must be some current information about it which can be retrieved and modified. In some countries difficulties have been experienced in obtaining accurate statistics about the size and cost of the civil service. Consequently, the number of ghost workers could not be ascertained and exact expenditure unknown because there is an inadequate information system in place.

Also, in Ghana, for instance some ministries and departments have duplicated their domains and responsibilities as was in the case of Ministry of Finance and Economic Development (MoFED) in Sierra Leone before the merger in 2007. One of the rationales for the reason for such duplication or overlap of records as being not properly stored. And information is not shared by ministries so that they know what each of them is doing. Thus duplicating does not only waste time and resources but also expensive in the sense that staff are paid for duplicating the function of other departments.

The main purpose of maintaining good management of public service records is to facilitate the development of new approach and understanding the importance of all recorded information and to use it as a meaningful tool in reforming the services. It also aims to build the bridges between policy-makers and consumers of services in improving their skills in understanding and using recorded information for the development process. In Sierra Leone, the public service is not properly equipped in the area of modern Information Technology. The management of information systems is yet at its rudimentary stage in some respect that there has been an overwhelming reliance on files and papers. The lack of adequate physical storage facilities tends to create nightmares for people who have to retrieve and use the information with accuracy and timeliness. This lack of storage systems cause difficulties in making decisions, and hence deter transparency, accountability and good governance in the country.

PART 1:
THEORETICAL CONCEPT OF RECORDS MANAGEMENT AND ARCHIVES ADMINISTRATION

1. INTRODUCTION

This part discusses the development of records management, the policies, guidelines and procedures; and principles and practices; the relationship between records and archives management profession; freedom of information and records management; and the reformation of records management programme in public sector organisations.

2. DEVELOPMENT OF RECORDS MANAGEMENT

The concept of records management emanated from information management which is stated in the United States Federal Government Report (USFGR) in response to the archival experience of other developed nations. Based on the concept of records management, the ISO 15489, 2001 standards were formulated which involved the following:

a) the act of setting policies and standards;
b) assigning responsibilities and authorities;
c) the establishment and promulgation of procedures and guidelines;
d) making provision for a range of services relating to the management and use of records;
e) designing, implementing, and administering specialized systems for managing records; and
f) integrating records management into business system and procedures.

However, there are some contradictions in these ISO standards which seem that the content was only on the life cycle management of records. It would have better if the ISO standard included the cost benefit of managing records and the motivation of records management practitioners.

The act of caring for records originally was done by each branch and agency of the US government which often culminated in the loss or destruction of records. In the United State of America (USA) and some other countries such as Sierra Leone, the chief official overseeing the operation of the National Archives and Records Administration is the Archivist. In 1934, R.D.W Connor was the first Archivist of the National Archives established by Congress. In the 1949 the National Archives was incorporated into the General Services Administration (GSA) which later became independent in 1985 as NARA. This prompted the National Archives to make financial contributions and establish a comprehensive programme of Archives administration rather than records administration. In this case records management is seen as a product of American experience during and after World War II. Since then it has contributed to national development of a country worldwide.

In Ghana until the1930s there was no formal records management programme in place. The government and other private businesses kept records in whatever form they felt appropriate without the benefit of retention schedules, disposition guidelines, and formal information life-cycle procedures. The government however, recognised that some controls needed to be implemented to manage the massive volume of Ghana's records. This gave birth to the National Archives in 1934, with the primary task of identifying records that should be retained as opposed to those that might be eligible for disposal. Before long, it became quite clear that the Ghana government would need a better, more efficient, more uniform way of generating, sorting and destroying its records. And so the concept of records management was born. It is evident that as the economy of Ghana continues to grow in the following years, specialized records management facilities began to emerge. During the 1970, two new developments led to the expansion of the records management industry. First computers were introduced to businesses and words processing software; documents could be produced at large quantities. Second, new legislation requires businesses to start retaining records for a certain period of time. These two factors even paved the way for greater level of records management. At first records management departments began to make use of electronic file storage. Again, in the 1980s two more new technological developments in records management and storage were introduced. First, barcodes and scanners were introduced. With these scanners, barcodes could be attached to files and boxes for identification later on. These improve the management control and security aspect of records management. The second new technological development was the compact disks (CD) which were capable of storing thousands of documents in a very small space. In the 1990s computer technology advanced again and led to greater efficiency gains for the records management filed. Thus, with the advent of digital scanners, paper document could be read and converted automatically into electronic files.

3. POLICIES, PROCEDURES AND GUIDELINES

Records are acknowledged as systematic management significance in order to protect and preserve them as evidence of actions, to support future activities and business decision and ensure accountability to present and future stakeholders and customers. This policy set out the procedures and practices needed to control and manage records efficiently and effectively. In developed countries these policies exist but are not efficiently and effectively utilised; and Africa and Asia countries are no exceptions. On this note some of the listed items of furniture, office equipment and supplies that can be used to protect and preserve records as evidence of action for improving records management operation include library cards; book shelves; computers and printers; copy machines; public announcement system; desk lamp; desk chairs; fax machines; desks; tables; shredders; supple cabinets; face dusk mask; diskette storage boxes; Papers, work gloves; box labels; file folders; Box tapes; three holes punch machines; staple machine; gums and removers; file charge-out; Lab coat and buildings. However, even if all the facilities are provided, when records are not properly organised the problems still remains unanswered.

Records management can only become a specialised business discipline provided there is a systematic analysis and control of recorded information which includes any recorded information created, received, maintained, or used by an organisation in accordance with its vision and mission. Records management is an area of business that deals with the step-by-step control of recorded information and this can only be possible if there is a trained and qualified records manager that manages these activities right from creation to disposition of recorded information in any format

4. RECORDS AND ARCHIVE MANAGEMENT PROFESSION

The act of records management is a professional discipline since the 1950s, although its concept and methods have been expanded and refined considerably. Currently, records management is a professional career with so many practitioners. The idea and practice is incorporated in so many disciplines such as Economics, Accounting, and Business management, Computing, Telecommunication, Knowledge Management, Information Science, Library Science, Archival Administration and Industrial Engineering. On this premises the similarities and differences of the archives and records management professions are as follows; For the similarities both

a) are called to identify which documents(records) they will manage;
b) need to be careful about maintaining the physical and intellectual integrity of the records in their care;
c) describe and arrange records to provide access as well as contextual information;
d) observe necessary legislation regarding disposal, privacy, intellectual property, and other issues; and
e) maintain the physical- including digital-condition of records.

Further, their differences could be based centrally on cultural, societal, and historical dimensions. Archives are political and cannot be seen only as preserving records for historical research or as warehouse for old records no longer in current administrative use. And records management, on the other hand, has emerged from modern capitalist idea of management in both government and non-governmental institutions. This means that there is efficiency, productivity, competitive advantage, and strategic value, increase of profit and avoidance of loss. Management of records as an integral part of business processes, is associated with workflow, and is based on administrative and legal necessity.

There has been a lot of debate among researchers about the discipline of Records Management being traditionally viewed with little significance. This argument continues today especially in developing countries such as Sierra Leone where records management for the past couple of years is yet to attain high level of attention and support that it receives in developed countries. In support of their argument registries and records management are not highly viewed as priority areas but frankly registries are managed by staff who has limited experience and managerial skills.

As Information Communication Technology (ICT) has expanded and presented opportunities for records keeping in developing countries. For instance, it enhanced retrieval systems and online search facilities. Opportunities for compact storage through electronic and digital storage devices are becoming more familiar to those responsible for records as they offer an alternative to bulky paper records that needs a considerable amount of space for storage facilities. And without records management policies to provide guidance to record creators and users of records pose severe risks that cannot be avoided. The Public Sector Reform taking place globally now put premium on accountability and transparency. Agencies are thus realizing the significance of records keeping as tools pivotal for good governance. The challenges facing developing countries in relation to archives and records are of the same. They include lack of resources, space constraints, high staff turnover, specific approaches to records and archives management. Two prominent issues need to be addressed for archives and records management to develop given the prestige that the profession deserves. These are the lack of accessible training programmes and the need for holistic and targeted awareness programmes at all administrative levels of any organisation, and the public in general.

A lot of arguments have been put up in conjunction with an integral relationship between archives and governmental efficiency, economic development, and national unity. In varied ways it can be perceived that records management and archives administration do make significant contributions to national development. There have been a lot of debate that administrative improvement is a "sine qua non" in the implementation of programmes of national development. The key to administrative advancement is the effective caring for information. Archival records should be preserved in facilities and equipment designed to ensure their permanent life, to discourage further deterioration, and to assure that the record maintain their utility condition. From the aforementioned, Ngulube (2006) highlighted that;

each new country has to establish its own special identity. It must select element of its history, culture, and act as symbols of national unity in public settings, on money, stamps, flags, government building, etc to show the people what they have in common as a united country and also what they can be proud of to possess together as a fellow countryman (p.108).

In this case a well organised archives office and good records management are paramount. If one could make comparison with other social sciences, archives studies still have a lot of gaps in the unknown area of research. Stakeholders including, head of states, governments, businesses or any group of people acting within society have to include within their priorities the provision of effective archives services. In this light, Carter (2006) observed that;

a country without archives will be something like a warrior without weapons, a doctor without tools to work with in the hospital. Public records are a solid ground on which the statesman can walk with security in order to conduct the affairs of a nation. They are the silent, important, impartial, reliable and external witness that bears testimony to the fortune, misfortune growth and the glories of the people (p.218).

Archival institutions serve as essential organs of public administration especially in developing countries fostering modern records management and requirement practices in government in enhancing administrative efficiency. Thus the regular deposit in an archival institution of rich stores of information, bearing on every aspect of national interest, which can be readily drawn upon for purposes of socio-economic development research hinges on proper records management. In this light the practical uses of archives are cultural resources; a mirror of the past; a collective national memory; and that a basic obligation of a community or a society is to preserve records of the past; and make them accessible to the public as cultural heritage.

It is true that records management programme intends to manage the life cycle of records effectively in order to ensure that:
a) records are known and are available to all the agency's staff who need to use them as supportive operation;
b) the transferring of records from their current stage is done as soon as they are no longer needed for active business; records are only kept by their creating agency if they still have historical value;
c) records with continued value are always protected from theft, fire, flood and other disasters;
d) records are stored in a secured environment with a minimum cost advantage; and
e) the life cycle of records is managed according to their stages.

In this light the process for managing records is frequently associated with living organisms as they can be reproduced, live and are being used, become aged/obsolescence and can be retired, died and taken to Archive institution for preservation. This premises maintained that records management provides a framework to enhance the following actions to be taken which include the:
a) currency of records;
b) accession of records;
c) interpretation of records;
d) trustworthiness of records;
e) timeliness of records;
f) dispositions of records as part of a plan and system.

Thus it is for this reasons that organisations with good records management practices benefit profusely in varied ways:
 a) the time of staff in filing and retrieving records is saved;
 b) decision-making and operation is enhanced with reliable and relevant record;
 c) the storage of record is always cost-effective when getting rid of obsolescence records;
 d) the demonstration of accountability is often with reliable evidence of policy, decision-making and action; and
 e) duplication of records is minimized in getting rid of duplicates and versions.

Further, the symptoms of poor records management are highlighted as follows:
 a) inaccurate information;
 b) out-dated information;
 c) duplication of records, not knowing the least version; complex filing systems difficult to use;
 d) waste of time looking for records and information when they are not properly organised;
 e) information is always prone to loss or damage; ubiquitous records;
 f) difficult to control records;
 g) waste of space due to unwanted storing of records;
 h) in-conducive working environment;
 i) poor decision making;
 j) user dissatisfaction;
 k) legislative requirement is not adhere to;
 l) Security is often lacking.

5. FREEDOM OF INFORMATION AND RECORDS MANAGEMENT

Archives and records management are based on the records series concept and two primary principles: records life cycle and records appraisal. In this case even legally enforceable right of access to information is meaningless if government records are not in proper order. Even when the information would be available in principle, if it cannot be found then it cannot be made available to citizens. This scenario cannot only limit government's accountability and their credibility in the eyes of citizens; it has a serious impact on the capacity of government to discharge its duties efficiently. It is evident that records management issues should be addressed by Freedom of Information (FOI) law and idea improvements implemented preceding its introduction. One of the provisions of most FOIs is that agencies must publish lists of record series they hold. A records series is a group of records or documents which may be filed and put together as a unit throughout their life cycle. Thus series must be organised and captured within the records keeping system. In addition to the requirements that the description of records are published, should be a commitment to the introduction of policies, standard and best practices as well as systems to ensure that information is managed through its life cycle.

This is to testify that without such procedures FOIs could be rarely successfully implemented. And sound archives and records management principles must be emulated if governments are to implement the requirement of access laws successfully. Poor records management practices should not be tolerated as an excuse for poor-decision making and sub-standard document searches. Records management is defined as the application of a systematic set of techniques to manage the records and documentation of an organisational unit. The objective is to ensure a proper creation, receipt, use, storage, short and long-term retention and disposal, their protection and maintenance, during and after their operational usefulness. Hence one could debunk that the importance of records management in today's Inforcentric world cannot be over emphasized. On this background, there need to be a national information policy in order to re-establish government's commitment towards its information infrastructure of which record management is a major component. Records management, like other information services, would be properly coordinated at policy level.

The aforementioned assertion could justify that the difference between information policy and creators of records in public sector institutions is very crucial. It could be acknowledged that the management and effective use of public records equally hinge on the effectiveness and efficiency of those mechanisms for processing the 'raw informational' material into utility products. In this direction, the civil service has a crucial role to play. The role of civil servants towards the proper organisation and utilisation of records cannot be underestimated. Thus the civil service is the brain power where policy decisions are generated in such a way that the establishment of the role of civil servants depicting the effective creation of records and consumption of these records as national resources by policy and decision makers will serve a manifestation of devotion. The truthfulness of the aforementioned proposition is prominently stated by Tough (2009) which emphasised that; *decision makers need records and archives when making decisions. The speed with which the decision is made and the quality of the decision taken hinges on the availability of good information which enhances all essential contributors to be considered before a decision is made (p.252).*

It is a plain fact that records created and managed in public institutions compose of a reliable memory of the government's past activities, thus functioning as repeated sequence of event memory for future activities. As Bunn (2009) succinctly posited; *public records serve as a tool which a civil servant can work with security in a constant exhausting labour in conducting the affairs of a nation. They bear witness to the testimony of the silent, impartial, reliable information to the labour, misfortunes, the growth and glories of the people (p.253).*

Some scholars of records management and archival administration argued that records allow continuity and consistency in administration as there utility indicates changes over a period of time. Virtually, records support the developmental planning and programmes of a nation. Democratically, records document government's responsibilities and accountability to the people. They make provision to a citizen with a sense of national identity and are of great beneficent to them in the establishment and protection of individual property rights and privileges.

In essence records provide a base for historical and biographical understanding. They also enhance orientation about the present and provide guidance for progress in the future. It has been a well-known fact that a key to administrative improvement is good records management, which is the handling of information towards a positive benefit of records as a national resource for development.

6. PRINCIPLES AND PRACTICES OF RECORDS MANAGEMENT

The principle and practice of records management have developed in response to information explosion engulfing modern work and the corresponding need for gradual approaches to the requirements of record keeping. These principles and practices are all imbedded in the policies of records management and archives administration in any organisation which Ministry of Finance and Economic Development (MoFED) Sierra Leone is no exception.

The perspective of Sierra Leone Government viewed record management as the process of planning, controlling, and directing, organising, training, promoting, and other managerial activities involved in the creation, maintenance and use, and disposition in order to achieve adequate and proper documentation of the policies and transaction of and its efficient and effective management of its Ministries, Departments and Agencies (MDAs) operations. The perspective of Ghanaian also stated that records management presupposes the act of identifying, classifying, archiving, preserving and destroying records. It's further defined as the field of management determining the systematic and efficient control of the creation, receipt, maintenance, use and disposition of records, which includes the process of capturing and maintaining evidence of information about business activities and transaction in the form of records. In this scenario, records management can be seen as a primary tool for identification and management of an organisation's evidence of business and non-business activities. In addendum to this view, the following points of records management practice are as follows:

a) creating, approving, and the enforcement of records policies which include classification system and the record retention policy;
b) the development of storage plan for both short and long-term deposit of physical records and digital information;
c) identification of current, semi and non-current record, classifying them according to standard operating procedures;
d) the coordination of access and circulation of records either within and even outside of the organisation; and
e) implementing the retention policy so as to achieve the destruction of records according to operational demands, procedures, statutes, and regulations (p.26).

However, records management field emanated from the archival profession during the 1950's and the proceeding years achieved a distinct professional identity in its own right. Nevertheless, the two professions still have identities in common, and records managers need a good understanding of archival principle and practice in order to develop a comprehensive records management programme. In the perspective of governments in the sub-Sahara African countries, the two professions are not far-fetched. They manage the same record media; both are concerned with the quality of records and they use the same system and techniques to augment their accessions. Thus the record life cycle model reveals that record managers must concern with:
a) creating record;
b) maintaining records;
c) retrieving records; and
d) disposition of records;

Archivists as well are concerned with:
a) identifying and selecting archives;
b) acquisition of archives;
c) arrangement and description;
d) preservation of archives and
e) provision of access.

In this scenario archives management programmes consist of a number of fundamental archival functions, the most significant could be appraisal, accessioning, preservation or conservation, arrangement and description and reference services for archival records. On this note, Archival functions are also extended to recruitment and training of records management practitioners. Their significance is highlighted by Kargbo (2015) who posited that: *archival records are a collection of historical documents of a government, a family, an organisation and also the place where government and other national records are kept and properly managed and administered. They could be of any type, shape or form such as maps, diary, reports and letters, or even computer tapes and print materials. They could be loose sheet or bound. Archival records have administrative and professional value for their creation agency or organisation (p.89).*

Since modern archivists appraise records and select those with enduring value, they must have an immense interest in records management. They must recognize that everything that records managers do or leave undone will directly or indirectly affect the archives in the future. Records managers profusely determine the quality of the archives, which means the completeness or adequacy of the documentation, its integrity and its accessibility for reference and research purposes. Records managers determine the nature of the archivists' work within modern archives, in which case the success of their effort depend on the ease or difficulty with which records can be appraised for disposition and can be selected for preservation; the ease or predicament which they can be arranged and described, made accessible and available for utilisation. It has been perceived that the interest of the modern archivist in records management is thus not often legitimate but paramount.

The early formation of records management identified specialisation and today there is a growing number of specialists at records centres, libraries, archives managing files, reports, directives, microfilms, source data, automation, machine-readable, scanners, tablets and the host of others in the arena of records management. Thus the concept of records management being a specialised subject of study and practice is a mere new discipline in African countries especially Sierra Leone. Though it is known in some countries but is seldom practised by many administrators as many organisations face problems in records management. Records and Information Management (RIM) is the professional practice of managing the records of organisation through their life cycle, from the time they are created to their eventual disposal. These include identifying, classifying, storing, securing, retrieving, tracking and destroying or permanently preserving records. This form of records includes paper records, voice records, x-rays and photographs as well as electronic records(e-mail, Google, Facebook, order forms, shipping notices). The control of such records will prevent the creation of irrelevant records and unnecessary extra copies, ensuring efficient, economical use of records in both the active and inactive periods, and destroy the records as soon as they are not needed. Thus records management motivates the efficient retrieval and use of information with minimum cost of records keeping. It can also be defined as the systematic control of all records from their creation or receipt, via processing, distribution, organisation, storing, and retrieval, to their ultimate disposition. This is further extended that records can be a tangible paper object or it can be in digital or electronic document form. These records can be kept on financial, medical, informative, formal documents, office documents, payroll, government forms and emails. Records management addresses the three phases of the life cycle of records. Thus the act of records management system enables the capturing, classification, and ongoing management of records throughout their life cycle. It could be both paper-based and computer system due to information explosion in this 21st century.

In the nutshell the definitions of records management can be put as being a logical act of creation, use, and disposition of records and the information they contain with minimum cost. Any organisation that institutes a cogent programme of records management can also manage the quality and quantity of that information it creates; and it can care for that information in a way that can provide effective services for its needs and can also dispose of the information when its usefulness is ended. It is clearly shown that records management is a professional discipline that deals with the creation, maintenance, and disposition of records. This management of records ranges from forms, reports, directives, active filing, inactive storage, record retention and varied components.

7. REFORMATION OF RECORDS MANAGEMENT PROGRAMME

Records management procedures in most public sectors have traditionally been shared among different institutions with little coordination. However since the institution of the reform programme in 1990, they made an apt observation, for example, in Ghana and discovered that the life cycle of public records has been partitioned into three phases: current, semi-current and non-current. There is an introduction of regulations under the ordinance which directs to the archivist to ensure that government's records are often transferred to the archives as and when necessary via the use of disposal schedules. The management of the second and third phases of the life cycle of public records is the responsibility of the national archives; maintaining that the first phase of public records logically falls within the domain of government offices but lacks professional guidance. A composed work provided by most public archives in developing countries had left enormous gaps between government offices, parastatal and private sectors respectively in concert with the advice and guidance in managing records. However, before the institution of reform programme traced the origins of the problems in records management which is ignited by the lack of a comprehensive policy aimed at an integrated holistic approach to the management of the whole life cycle records. In this case records management has rendered many African countries so problematic with minimal or no co-ordination. This emphasized the fact of the situation as being aggravated by the lack of adequate professional staff to cope with the mere volume of work. Since then, the lack of functional records centres has put a lot of pressure on the storage resources of registries; this had made the semi-current phase of the records life cycle suffer most. Coupled with the lack of comprehensive retention schedules, the absence of national records centres has a further big blow on the records transfer and machinery, culminating into an obstructive of very expensive registry storage space with inactive records. Thus the incapability of staff that is neither trained nor motivated results in the lack of proper control over the quantity and quality of paper work during that period.

This reform programme has brought on board enormous capital injection into the records management which enable an overhaul of the system. All registries in the public sector were restructured, a new legislative framework was put in place, a functional records centre was restructured, and omnibus retention schedule was reviewed and a number of records staff were trained and re-trained. It was however discovered that "Act 535, having been in operation for seventeen(17) years, needed regulation to make it more operational, has not yet been put in place"(p.186). It is hoped that with adequate funding and structural support, the new system will be sustained to the benefit of efficiency and productivity of the Ghana public sector.

The primary function of records management is to facilitate the free flow of records through an organisation to ensure that information is available rapidly where and when it is needed. To carry out this function needs an efficient and effective records management programme. In helping users do their jobs better and more easily, the records manager should do that accordingly. Any organisation established, private or public, should document its activities and this can only be done by creating records. Records contain information relating to an organisation's activities captured in reproduction during the organisation course of administration. Records display and confirm the decision taken, the actions carried out and the result of such action. "They support policy and management decision-making, protect the interest of the organisations, the right of the employers, clients' citizens and help the organisations to conduct its business and deliver its services in consistent and equitable manner"(p.15). Records management is critical to all organisations: unless records are managed efficiently, it is not possible to conduct business, to account for what has happened in the past or to make decisions about the future. In this light, records are vital corporate assets and are required to provide evidence of actions and decisions. Ho Polytechnic as a tertiary institution in Ghana did practice sound records management. The institution's records management is shifting from manual to electronic system of managing by using computers and internet. Thus this allows users to complete and submit the information on time. The electronic filing system prevents the users from making serious mistakes that could affect the operation and image of the institution.

Records management is the activities of a one-man operation up to multi-national entity and the central departments of governments all have the need to keep good records, as they provide evidence of the activities undertaken. The first thing to encounter in caring for records is the problem of management. It is clearly evident that the pay-off including the effectiveness and even cost-efficient is not always known to the organisational entity and those who control it. Strategically records management aims to uncover a clear analysis of all the information resources being created internally in the organisation; then making up with other major information generation entities such as libraries so as to device an intelligible information strategy. Procedurally, records management aspires to achieve effective documentation of the organisational entity policies, procedures and business transactions, and making these records accessible to those urgently and effectively in need of them. The procedure can also be considered as getting the right record to the right person at the time the information is needed and at minimal cost.

The strategic benefits of effectively managing financial, managerial, social corporate records rest on good records management. Good records management is all about having knowledge and comply with the legal requirement affecting the creation, retention of corporate records. In conclusion it is necessary to have qualities of a disciplined approach to managing corporate records. Good records caring must be achievable, accessible, manageable, and comprehensible. In order to attain, commitment to the whole programme by senior management, must be the most significant priority within the organisation. Saving and risk management (cost reduction, cost avoidance, productivity, and effectiveness) has to be the next most priority to consider instead of concentrating on resource costs of introducing new programme or buying more facilities and equipment and supplies and perhaps new staff to run the organisation. It is also true that there are a lot of variables affecting the way offices make their equipment selection and these include factors ranging from cost, required floor space to appearance and office aesthetics and each office should have a unique system. These capabilities of different types of equipment must be measured in the context of those unique systems in order to reduce cost. Good records management has to be simple in order to achieve an organisation's goal. It is always possible to choose broadly based programmes with immense advantage rather than embarking on the modification of current products. Finally, an organisation's records management system needs to be straightforward and comprehensible, and the people who will use them need good and apt training. With these basic elements in place will at least be a right starting point. However it is good that training, and emolument/salary of the records management and archives practitioner be in tandem with other information and non- information professionals in order to bridge income disparity in profession. For many years there have been a debate and discussion on the subject of the relationship between the conceptual framework of archives administration and records management which varied authors see it as a research ground.

PART 2:
THE MANAGEMENT OF PUBLIC SECTOR FINANCIAL RECORDS

1. INTRODUCTION

This part of literature discusses the management of public sector financial records keeping in enhancing transparency, accountability and good governance for sustainable development in public sectors organisations. A financial record keeping is viewed as bedrock for achieving national development in Africa. Ordinary Africans are often requesting financial accountability and transparency and sustainable development from their leaders and financial managers. These demands by citizens and leaders for great openness and financial accountability have also been joined by international donors. Thus a proper system of financial records keeping has become an integral part of managing public sector financial organisations in today's competitive and challenging business environment. A good financial records keeping enables organisations to plan properly and also check for misappropriations of resources.

2. FINANCIAL RECORDS MANAGEMENT POLICY

Financial records management policy is a policy that guide the way financial records should be managed. Developing and implementing a financial records management policy requires clarity about its aims and objectives irrespective of whether the system is manual or electronic thus:

a) maintaining the financial records throughout their life in a consistent and structured manner;
b) supporting the audit function and external accountability of the organisation;
c) enabling the organisation to meet its legislated financial obligations;

d) meeting the accounting, reporting and financial management need of the organisation, including economic and fiscal policy and planning;
e) protecting the integrity and accuracy of records to guarantee the organisation a reliable source of financial information;
f) providing ready access to and retrieval of, financial information;
g) making cost-effective use of resources allocated to the creation, maintenance and use of financial records, thus ensuring timely disposal of records without compromising their integrity and utility as an information resource;
h) adding value to financial system through documentation and control of financial records; and
i) Training and salary payment of staff.

Financial records series can be controlled from the time they are created and maintain throughout their life. Within each series, there is usually a further level of control over individual records items. There may be for example, serial numbered vouchers, checks or forms classified by account codes or a chronological arrangement of documents by financial years or monthly accounting periods. Information about the records series can be recorded in a register of records series held in each agency. Such a register would record essential contextual information about a series. This contextual information should include:
a) title and description;
b) date range;
c) creating agency;
d) system of arrangement and control;
e) records format;
f) related legislation/financial instruction;
g) related accounting manual procedure;
h) storage location; and
i) Disposal authority (p.33).

However, a number of principles could be applied to the process of identifying financial records which could be easily retrieved for decision

making in enhancing accountability and good governance in public sector financial institutions. Thus:
a) where more than one volume of records are created in a financial year each volume should be given a single sequential number(1,2,3 and so on) with the sequence starting again at the beginning of each financial year;
b) the main component of financial systems will be accounting records, which should be created and maintained as discrete records series;
c) each item should be part of a clearly defined series;
d) some types of financial records are retained in a general filing system. These may include policy documents, authorities such as warrants, budget papers, tenders, contracts and project documentation. The organisation's registry or records office should play a role in their management. In a decentralised organisation the files may also be managed by sub-units secretaries, who should take account of financial information management requirements; and
e) in order to identify records in a consistent way, file titles should use terms obtained from a master list of authorized terms. File titles should also include the financial year and, where appropriate, the accounting code. For example: WARRANT-VIREMENT-1995/96 AND EXPENDITURE-MONITOR-1995/96-SUB-HEAD 021(p.35).

3. FINANCIAL INFORMATION/RECORDS

Financial information is information in the form of numbers portraying the income and expenditure of an organisation. Management of proper financial records is essential to the growth and survival of organisations. In order to ensure efficiency, effectiveness and the continuity survival of public and private sector organisations, management must seek for reliable, relevant, accurate and timely financial information for planning and decision making. These financial information includes financial policies; annual budget reports/financial statements; payrolls; payment voucher; purchase orders; requisition and store ledgers; payment requests and receipts; ledgers; cash books; journals; bank statements and deposit slips; stock sheets; invoices; credit notes; computer records; bills of entry; consignment notes; and any other financial records. Poor management of financial records will lead to resources mismanagement and poor cash management and this can cause the organisation to collapse. Poor record keeping makes it difficult to differentiate between organisational and personal assets, and it is the responsibility of stakeholders to avoid using assets of the organisation for personal transaction. , A well-qualified Accountant and records manager should be employed to manage financial records. Records managers and financial managers should work in tandem as both of them should have proper knowledge to control cash, as liquidity is a key to the success of a public sector organisation. Both financial and records managers play a pivotal role in decision making process of any organisation. With their skills and experiences, they are in a greater position to measure the financial performance and position of an organisation. This allows users especially management to plan and make economic decisions. On this note, non-financial and financial records are managed in the same way; the only difference is some financial records have shorter lives than the other records. They can be appraised, have a retention period ranging from 1-6 years and can be archived for future use. The retention period for most financial records is 1, 2 and 6 years respectively before taking to the archives or destroyed. They should also be managed according to regulatory framework of records management. However, in some organisations, there are many financial records that have lived over six years still as current records. This can only be done when its importance is still needed.

To buttress the foregoing explanation, the general principles of financial records management which any organisation should adhere to managing financial records are thus:
   a) managing financial records is the joint responsibility of accounting, audit, financial and records personnel;
   b) financial records should be managed throughout their life, from the point of creation to their ultimate disposition;

c) financial records should be arranged to permit their retrieval by accounting periods and by financial activity;
d) financial records should be protected against unauthorized access, alteration, copying and destruction;
e) control should be exercised over the structure, content, location and movement of financial records;
f) financial records are retained for the length of time required to meet statutory obligations and the need for financial operation, management, audit and research;
g) and financial records and records systems should be subject to audit and review with the objective of minimizing records management cost.

For this reasons records give an evidence of transactions, noting that well-managed records provide sound base for financial and accounting control and hence accountability. Records also provide the basis for financial reporting. He observed that the ability of a state to create, sustain, and promote development hinges on the ability of the state to manage recorded information about the conduct of government financial business activities as the most significant venture. And without a records management programme in place, it is hard to provide an evidence of financial management activities because they are disorganised and missing. In this light financial records management requires the systematic control, authorised storage and disposal of financial records. When records are not effectively structured, there will be difficulty in acquiring information. Thus, records management is the pillar that determines the financial management process and makes provision for the government to make meaningful social, economic and political decision with great commitment to prove state accountability. If the link between recorded information and financial management process is not intensified, the general principle of financial records management, will lead to the inability of the government to achieve its ultimate goal in which, will be advisable to : improve the effectiveness of public expenditure programmes; manage external resources; mobilize domestic resources; manage the size and efficiency of the public sector; adjust to changing macro and micro- economic conditions; expenditure control; cash management; auditing and the dissemination of information within government and to the private sector. However, the effective management of public sector financial information is a critical factor in providing capacity for public sector efficiency and governance. This view supports an emerging trend in public sector management system which provides the evidence required to support transparency and accountability and at the same time inform the effective management of the consolidated fund. And without documentary evidence or following the principles aforementioned, the public has no means of holding the state accountable. In effect public financial records provide an effective means by which the public measure the full performance of their government.

4. FINANCIAL RECORDS MANAGEMENT AND ACCOUNTABILITY

Accountability is defined as a process that allows people to measure and verify the performance of government. Financial accountability is a critical component of an accountable government. It involves legislative control of executive through budgets and accounts. Weakness in financial accountability is generally linked to poor cash management, auditing, and the management of financial records. Thus an enhanced level of control over financial management is pivotal for all governments to maintain their commitment to citizens. Financial management ensures that money is allocated in accordance with the government's strategic priorities. This is achieved by controlling the budget approved by the legislation and is enforced by the publication of audited accounts of what was actually spent. This has made public sector financial management the focus in recent years. Reduction in public expenditures has pressured public authorities to maintain services with less money. To achieve cuts, financial managers have had to improve their financial analysis as a basis for improving efficiency and value for money. Thus good public management and administration with emphasis on accountability and responsiveness to consumers' needs has been seen as an aspect of good governance.

It is a truism that without reliable, authentic documentary evidence government cannot demonstrate to society of the use of public resources responsibly and that it has fulfilled its mandate to the people. One may be convinced that the loss of control of the official evidence base in public financial management is one of the most minimum organised threats to accountability and the government. Also, the lack of accountability in the management of records poses implication for government efficiency. Thus, without evidence of financial management, accountability initiative cannot be archived. In essence the barometer of good government is 'financial records' and the way by which these records are processed and maintained to serve as evidence of good government is 'financial records keeping.' And without records there cannot be demonstration of accountability, and without evidence of accountability, society hardly trusts in public institutions. In this scenario, it should be deduced that the relationship between financial records and accountability are two sides of a coin which are the main pillars of good governance. Against this backdrop, there are other verifiable evidence in ascertaining accountability and transparency apart from financial records such as local publications, business journals, financial bulletins, and financial journals.

In this day and age despite the introduction of computerisation, the volume of financial information and records in most organisations continue to grow. The appropriate and timely disposal of these records is an essential aspect of managing financial records. In this case appraisal, retention and disposition systems are the centre of accountability. As financial records are found throughout an organisation, the planning, appraisal and implementation of the disposal process requires co-operation and co-ordination throughout the organisation to ensure that audit trials and the evidential qualities of records are maintained while the volume of records is controlled. Appraisal involves determining these records worthy of ongoing retention because of their utility value. The following issues should be taken into account in apprising financial records:

a) Legislation and regulations may contain requirements for the retention and disposal of records. Particularly relevant are laws relating to finance, customs, and excise duties, taxation, pensions, social security, employment and audit. Also important are statutes concerning evidence and limitation on action for claims. For example statutes bearing for accounting records may include Civil Evidence Acts, Value Added Tax, Companies Act, Consumer Protection Act, Data Protection Act, Financial Service Act and the Limitation Act.

b) Financial records may provide the creating organisation with valuable administrative, legal and fiscal evidence. Knowledge of the administrative context in which the records were created, including an understanding of financial system and the functional relationships of records, is required for a proper assessment of their values.

c) The records may also provide valuable information of wider research interests for example, research into political, economic and social activities has demonstrated a key interest in the long term preservation of financial records.

d) The cost of retention and the availability of resources should be considered when appraising records. Cost is the critical factor given the volume of many series of financial records and the technological support required for electronic records.

e) The utility of records should be considered. The utility of records is depended on their completeness, accuracy, arrangement, physical condition and accessibility.

f) Aggregate financial information may provide more information in less space than other records. Financial records may comprise summaries, consolidated accounts, annual statements, statistics and reports.

g) Financial records may be duplicated. The duplication of transaction records is a common feature of manual or mixed financial records keeping system because of the need to keep different stakeholders informed.

However, financial institutions in Sierra Leone are aware of the aforementioned Acts and regulations governing financial management. But records management has never been a priority. This is because there is no enforcement of practice. For organisations failing to produce records/documents on request, the maximum penalty for being guilty for an offence (as stated in a company's Acts) is fined five hundred thousand Leone (Le.500,000) (approximately equivalent to $50 dollar). In this case, it is evident that records management could give huge benefits and merits; many do not take appropriate steps as the need is not pressing and the penalty is not too severe.

5. MONITORING AND COMPLIANCE

Monitoring and compliance is the act of checking whether or not the policies, principle and practice of financial and non-financial records keeping is actually adopted in an organisations. The programme for managing financial records should be monitored on a regular basis. Monitoring should be carried out according to an agreed programme to ensure the continued evidential and legal accountability of an organisation's financial records management system and continuing effectiveness. Monitoring process must be documented to provide evidence of compliance with policies, procedures, and standards for managing records adopted by an organisation. It stated that the records centre of an organisation should have a regular programme for monitoring records management systems and procedures. In addition, national records and archival institutions should carry out regular records management inspection against an agreed plan, as set out in records and archives legislation. This should include a systematic inspection of records managed by financial services in line ministries to ensure compliance with records management procedures and policies, identifying areas of strength and weakness and measuring performance. On this note, the report of Auditor General also affects the management of financial records in institutions, and records management audit/inspection should be carried out on financial records at regular intervals, two or three times a year. However, the guidance provides draws on the methodology used by them. The national records and archive institution should build up central inspection files covering:

a) primary and secondary legislation affecting financial records(e.g, public records legislation, financial legislation, data protecting legislation);
b) financial regulations and procedures(e.g, financial instructions, accounting manual);
c) records keeping regulations and procedures(e.g, record inventories, records schedules, disaster plan, registry instructions, registry list, appraisal criteria);
d) organisation chats(including all locations of the Ministry of Finance and line ministries);
e) listing of key financial and records staff(i.e. posts in ministries);
f) main computerised system and locations(with diagram if available); and
g) annual inspection reports for previous years.

Also, external monitoring by the national records and archives institution should be conducted across governments according to an agreed inspection plan. This will provide for a cycle of inspection as allowed by resources. It is unlikely that all agencies are inspected every year. Agencies with weak systems should be targeted for follow-up inspection to access the effectiveness of remedial action in strengthening records system. The central inspection working file should be set up listing: inspection objectives and inspection plan; resources questionnaire; and control test and result. However, in some developing countries, such as South Africa National Archive and Records Services (NARSSA) does compliance monitoring programme in receiving and inspecting different aspects of the performance of the records control system. This includes the following:
a) inspection to ensure that records identified are being properly created and captured in financial records management system;
b) inspection to ensure the proper implementation of user permission and security procedure;
c) tracking of work flow processes via sampling to ensure adherence to policies and procedures;

d) inspection to ensure that records are being retained as laid out in disposal authorities; and
e) inspection of documentation of records destroyed or transferred to determine whether or not destruction/transferred was authorised in accordance with disposal inspection and that the documentation meets the required standard.

The delegation of compliance monitoring can also be carried out by an internal audit of organisations and other units rather than national records and archives institutions. The focal point is that compliance monitoring must be done on a regular basis and a vital records protection programme will protect against some disasters and lessen the damage of others, but disasters will still happen and the results can be devastating ,to an organisation unless it has implemented policies and procedures to protect its records. When a disaster does occur there must be a disaster recovery programme designed to:

a) minimize disruption of normal financial operations;
b) prevent further escalation of this disruption;
c) minimize the economic impact of the disaster;
d) establish alternative operating procedures;
e) train personnel in emergency procedures;
f) recover/salvage organisational assets; and
g) provide for rapid and smooth restoration of service.

A disaster recovery programme should consist of three parts: prevention, preparation and recovery. And a disaster team should be appointed to: ensure that efforts are made to prevent potential disaster; provide documentation of the organisation's readiness to respond to a disaster; and provide information on recovery procedures and cost. On this note a disaster plan should be prepared, updated regularly and disseminated widely. The document would serve as a tool for communicating the disaster prevention and recovery plan within the organisation, and must be developed in co-ordination with all staff involved with handling emergencies within the organisation. Senior management should approve the disaster plan. Staff must understand their roles and functions and be comfortable with those tasks. Thus they should receive training and updates on a regular basis so that their response is automatic. Most of the organisations including the Labour Organisation/Trade Union do not have a disaster recovery programme on financial records management and public sector organisation in Sierra Leone is no exception to this anomaly.

It is evident that any control system for monitoring records is only as effective as the people who run and contribute to it. This is true for financial records where stakeholders come from both the records and accounting staff that will play their pivotal role in managing financial records in achieving good governance in public sector organisation to be specific. As for many areas, managing human resources in a system for keeping financial records is about ensuring that the right people are in the right place in their right numbers and with the right skills. Three areas have been identified as contributing factors namely: an adequate career structure; defined competencies for different roles; and sufficient and appropriate training.

Auditing is part of monitoring which can support national development and government good will. Supreme Audit Institution (SAI), such as offices of Auditor General, publish consolidated reports on audit outcomes for local authorities, government, departments, parastatals and related public entities. These reports identify broad areas analysed during audit exercises that often include financial management, governance, asset management, risk management, revenue collection and debt recovery. They highlight trends that were detected during audit exercise at the end of the financial year. In essence, records management affect audit exercises as well as financial management within audited institutions. A records management audit should be carried out of financial records at random intervals two or three times a year. The audit or inspection should check that records management procedures are understood and are being carried out consistently. It can be undertaken more frequently when computerised accounting applications are in use and provide for audit trial. This audit can be performed by the internal

audit unit or by the records authority. Hence this noted audit should check that:
a) the financial records required by law and internal regulations are maintained and readily accessible;
b) standard disposal actions have been carried out under approved disposal authority(p.4).

However, copies of the audit reports should be forwarded to the authority and accountable head of the agency, who should be able to take responsibility for ensuring that appropriate action is taken on any recommendation made. The audit report provides a basis for action where a records problem is identified. It should be particularly useful to accounting officers, who are responsible for producing and maintaining financial records, and to the head of the Ministry of Finance, who has a broad policy responsibility for the operations of the government's financial and accounting system (p.7). However, there is a strong correlation between records management concerns and audit opinions raised by Comptroller and Auditor General of Zimbabwe's (CAGZ's) narrative audit reports. Inadequate records management within government entities was associated with adverse and qualified opinions and, in some cases, unqualified opinions that have emphasis of matters. There is a causal loop in which lack of documentary evidence of financial activities was the source cause of poor accounting and poor auditing reports. Any error resulting from inaccurate or in-complete records meant that government entities were not showing a true picture of their financial status and their financial statements could be materially misstated. Thus as an important monitoring and control system, records management should be integrated into the accounting and auditing processes of government entities.

6. FINANCIAL MANAGEMENT AND RECORDS MANAGEMENT

Financial management involves planning, controlling, implementing and monitoring fiscal policies and activities, including accounting and auditing revenue, expenditure, asset and liability. It entails daily cash management as well as the formulation of short, medium and long-term financial objectives, policies and strategies in support of the organisation's business. Financial management also includes planning and controlling capital expenditure, managing assets, liaising with the treasury and making decision relating to funding and performance. Thus good financial management is critical to the success of an organisation, whatever its size and whether or not it is in the public, private or voluntary sectors. Financial records are produced in every area of financial management. If these records are not well managed, the financial function suffers. Thus, financial records management and records management are closely related. The breakdown of a financial system is often related to that in records management. As people rarely make the link between problems in financial management and inadequacies in the way records are managed, yet records are the sources of all the information used in financial management systems. And if records become so disorganised that it is difficult or impossible to audit properly, the long term effect will be that fraud or errors will not be detected or corrected. When a system of financial management breaks down, the consequences are serious. Thus:

a) monitoring systems are inadequate and information is difficult to access;
b) vote ledgers are not kept properly, important tool for financial control is lost;
c) accounts are not produced on time, rendering them of limited value for expenditure control and monitoring; and
d) audit system is ineffective.(p.1)

In this light, the distinction between records management and financial management could be: records management reinforces financial control and support accountability and transparency. The ability to reveal who did what, why and how is a powerful means of deterring individuals from engaging in fraud or corruption thus enforcing accountability. Well managed records, provides an unbiased account of responsibility and reliability. Authentic and reliable records provide the unambiguous link between the authority to carry out a transaction, the particular individual concerned and the date. Records can identify abuse, misuse and non-compliance with financial institutions. While financial management also hinges upon a system of internal control that makes it possible to carry out business in an orderly and efficient manner; ensure adherence to management policies and safeguard assets; and the management of financial records is a key component of this control system. Where financial records are not controlled, their completeness and accuracy cannot be guaranteed. Records needed for reference, decision making and risk assessment can become difficult to access. The senior officials responsible for accounting, such as Accountant General, Financial Secretary, the Minister of Finance normally issue detailed regulations for the control of financial management systems. Complete and accurate records must be available to prove that these controls are functioning properly and consistently. In essence these records, if properly controlled, help to ensure that their context, content and structure are intact.

On this note, records management is a supportive tool to executing accounting and auditing functions. Financial records keeping provide a basis for accounting and introduce controls that protect essential audit trials. At the most practical level if records are not organised, it will take auditors an excessive amount of time to locate needed documents, if they can find them at all. Individuals guilty of embezzlement may deliberately allow financial records to become disorganized or to be stored in unsuitable conditions because this makes harder for auditors to identify fraud.

On the other hand, in some cases government officials have been inappropriately accused of embezzling funds simply because the documents portraying the expenditure could not be located. Well-managed records are essential to overcome economic crime and protect the innocent. A financial records management programme should enable the physical and logical control of records and prevent unauthorized access, tempering, loss or destruction, be it intentional and accidental. Records management should contribute a layer of security and reassurance that operations are in financial management systems. In reality, records management, accounting, and auditing provide the layer of control that is essential to ensuring transparency, probity and integrity in financial management system.

Sierra Leone, a developing country cannot ensure accountability and transparency and operationalize Right to Access Information (RAI) or the Open Government Initiative (OGI) in the current condition. If for example RAI, is emphasizing access to records, public sector organisations need to properly manage their records before access is possible. Thus until these possible problems should be addressed such as:
a) amend the current Archives Law;
b) ensure at least a records Centre in each of the four regions of the country;
c) embark on clearing of massive backlog of closed files and other documents currently occupying expensive office space across the public service;
d) work towards improved records management cadre;
e) restructure records office systems across the public service;
f) produce retention schedules for various types of records(example, financial, human resources, health and legal; and;
g) training for records staff on the hybrid(paper and electronic environment).

And without access to information there is no transparency; without transparency, accountability cannot be expected; and without accountability and transparency democratic credentials are incomplete.

7. FINANCIAL RECORDS KEEPING AND INFORMATION TECHNOLOGY (IT)

It is real that the preservation of records is a vital exercise in an organisation and with the advent of technology; electronic information has introduced new preservation requirements. This is reducing the use of paper based information to the use of materials such as tapes, magnetics discs, optical discs, for preserving or storing information and how to technically preserve electronic records indefinitely; how to choose what to preserve; and how to guarantee electronic records reliability and authenticity in future. Proper management of financial records can make significant contribution to the organisation records management system by ensuring that information is available to take decisions and to protect inaccurate payments. Digital preservation has become more important as many organisations have realised that they need to keep data larger for regulating business activities. It highlights the areas which have to be improved to enable the digitisation of records take effect as soon as possible. Financial records are an important source of information for financial transactions as they were specifically used to document an organisation's expenses. Organisations faced a number of problems, the major being, the lack of policies, standard procedures and guidelines to underpin the effective and efficient management of financial records. Other issues included low priority accorded to records management; absence of records management culture; and inadequate skills for managing records especially electronic records format.

8. COMPETENCY AND EXPERIENCE IN MANAGING RECORDS

In many countries such as the Republic of South Africa, the function of managing current, semi-current records and archives is separated and falls to both accounting and records staff. This can be further divided into central agencies e.g. the national records and archive institutions and the Ministry of Finance, Treasury, and line ministry staff in both the records and accounting cadres. It is important for the effective functioning of the records management system that those staff with responsibility for managing records have a clear career path with appropriate grades and remuneration. The central government schemes of service provide guidance to the appropriate grades of staff employed. Thus there should be separate schemes of service for accounting and records staff as the two functions are very different. There should also be adequate numbers of staff to carry out the tasks for managing financial records. The number of posts will of course depend on the size of the organisation and the scope of the financial management system. A simple example of this is the position of records managers in line ministries. This is an important role for co-ordinating records management throughout the line ministries and liaising with the national records and archive institutions. However in small organisations it may be more appropriate to allocate these duties to suitably qualified individuals.

On the other hand, defined competence could make possible to identify required educational standards, training needs, level of experience and, whenever possible, practical expertise required by staff responsible for managing financial records. Where there is a relevant scheme of service in place of records staff, job specification must incorporate the qualifications specified by the scheme. It is also noted that the roles of records and accounts staff are dealt with only in relation to their responsibility for managing financial records. The competencies of each grade level, in terms of their responsibilities, entry qualifications, career development and training requirements should be defined carefully and clearly. For both records and accounting staff an important concept is that staff exercising the same levels of responsibilities should form part of the same grade. Thus the number of grades will depend on local practice, but four level of responsibility can be identified based on accountability, authority, and freedom to act independently:
   a) senior management responsible for the whole area of management and policy(e.g. Director of national records and archive institution);
   b) middle management responsible for planning policies and strategies across a large areas of work with the ability to change procedure across that area(e.g. a senior accountant);
   c) supervisory level exercises some initiative in responding to the needs of each new situation(e.g. records office supervisor); and
   d) operational level almost wholly under instructions (e.g. a registry clerk).

However, induction training should be provided in a timely fashion to all civil servants. The basic guidance on the rule and regulations governing the creation and handling of records, particularly the legal responsibilities conferred on all staff by the National Records and

Archives Act should be included. In addition, records staff should receive more detailed guidance in their induction training to help them understand the structure and duties of the government records management system. Accounting staff should also receive guidance in the day-to-day management of financial records. On-going training should be available to staff involved in managing financial records to help them in the performance of their duties and to help their career development. Notwithstanding, it is imperative to provide formal training in the theory and practice of records management to staff of an appropriate level in addition to on-the-job training. This enables records managers to gain an understanding of the importance of their role in supporting government objectives. In addendum to technical training, there should be training that provides management and supervisory skills necessary to successfully manage and supervise staff. This is as important as improving skills in records management. In this regard formal training is necessitated and should not be expensive. Thus the training course should be offered by the following:

a) the national records and archives institution;
b) civil service training college(e.g. Fourah Bay College, University of Sierra Leone offers courses in Library, Archive and Information Studies);
c) regional institutions; and
d) international courses(p.50).

For international courses, sending staff overseas for training is an expensive option and could be considered only if there is no suitable training available locally as it was in the case in Sierra Leone during 1960s and 1970s before the introduction of the course in question. It is important that staff receive high quality training. In this case there should be some means of assessing staff participating in training course to ensure that they have acquired the skills taught to a satisfactory level. This could be used for promotion so that their professional development is awarded. Against this background many developing countries with special reference to Sierra Leone do not have well-defined policies between records and accounting staff in relation to adequate career structure; competencies for different role; and sufficient and appropriate training for the management of financial records. However, if there are policies, procedures, their implementation could pose a threat to managing financial records in these countries. This is because of the lack of recognition for records professionals which they think are not important because the accountants/financial managers themselves can do the role of records managers. Thus Africans' mentality towards financial records management is another challenge for poor management of resources and the aftermath is financial unaccountability and bad governance.

In conclusion, many developing countries including Sierra Leone witness a vast breakdown of financial records keeping system in the public service. One could fervently argue that most of the financial records keeping problems and challenges discussed in this review are reflective of the public service in Sierra Leone. In this light, financial records keeping in a financial management system has been deteriorated across all areas of government now-a-days; there are also huge gaps in financial records but similarly vast quantities of inactive records, occupy some expensive office space in government buildings. Justifiably, it has been expressed that government information is in a chaotic state due to lack of recognition of information as a national resource. It is a truism that a breakdown in financial system is a breakdown in records management; the discontinuity of government decision and the distortion of national development has been emanated from poor management of financial records in enhancing accountability and transparency.

PART 3:
THE MANAGEMENT OF ELECTRONIC RECORDS

1. INTRODUCTION

This part introduces the definition and types of electronic records management system; the policies, procedures and guidelines in managing electronic records; challenges facing in managing electronic records; the relationship between information specialist and records managers in managing electronic records; and the importance of managing electronic records system in both Africa and beyond.

2. DEFINITIONS AND TYPES OF ELECTRONIC RECORDS

Electronic records are records in the form of software system in a computer waiting to be printed. An electronic record is that created, generated, sent, communicated, received or stored by electronic means that can require some form of computer technology to access and use. The definition of electronic records is synonymous and the use of computer is its most significant characteristic. Electronic records thus encompass all information concerning activities and processes in organisation that are generated electronically. Electronic records systems are the sum of all machineries that allow for the reading and manipulations of records such as electronic media as well as all connected items such as some documented output information, software application, programme and metadata. In this light, electronic records bring a fundamental and unique dimension to electronic records should maintain a basic nature of a records property that makes it reliable and trustworthy. To maintain these principles in records has become one of the greatest challenges in the records management platform particularly due to their lack of involvement in establishing computer technological innovations. However there are five main technical issues linked with electronic records in this 21st century: the storage media; hardware and software; data exchange standards; record keeping integrating systems;

and access and security. The event also showed case products like e-discovery, records and information policies, applications and technologies etc. In fact, the technical issues of security and access which naturally leads to the consideration of legal issues are often associated with electronic record.

Electronic records management is defined as the use of electronic equipment in creating, communicating, and maintaining records. This equipment documents government activities and decision making and ensures accountability. However, not all records in electronic format are records. A record should be in the structured form of information with content, context specific and may be held in a long storage medium. Thus, the use of computers makes the documentation and preservation of records more complex. And some electronic records would never be found on paper. In reality the transfer of electronic records to archive is hardly to be in existence in most African countries, not excluding Sierra Leone. Thus the modification of traditional records management and archives practice must be achieved in order to ignore the predicament of unauthorised disposal of computerised records. The termination of this practice must certify that "there is a maintenance of the integrity of records; non-irretrievability of records; only authorised records disposal occurs according to established records schedules; records having long term value can be easily channelled to another to an archive facility" (p.8).

It is necessary to adopt a continuum records management process in order to achieve a well-functioning of effective and efficient electronic records management system. A record has three characteristics, namely: content, context and structure. these characteristics refers content as a substance of a message; with regards to context it gives prudent information about a business function and activity for the purpose it was created; structure denotes format, a relationship between data element and the documented activities of the institution. It could be debatably asserted that these feature elements can affect the management and use of records within an arena of electronic records keeping system. They can also enhance the overhauling of records in the electronic form in which they have been created, thus promoting the convenient use of electronic records.

Electronic records show the way business is conducted, decisions taken and work executed. They are evidence of decisions, and actions. The same fundamental records management principles are apply to electronic records and other record formats. The technical nature of electronic records is a management challenge. Certain electronic records are identified such as e-mail, voicemail, geographic information system(GIS), Web-pages, work process document, spreadsheet, database, digital image, and video and audio files. They can be stored on optical discs, magnetic tape, diskettes, memory sticks, and a number of media. But electronic records face serious threats from technological wear-out due to rapid advancement of computer technology that can deter record accessible as a result of lack of planning.

3. CHALLENGES OF MANAGING ELECTRONIC RECORDS

The foremost challenging issue is to conduct a research before starting electronic records management programme. Visibility studies require collecting data on all records which include electronic records system, analysing and use for planning. The most effective technique to organising electronic records is to attain a filing system that reflects paper files. It is crystal clear that long term preservation is the most challenging task of managing electronic records. The most effective labour intensive and costly solution is to relocate data periodically to a new software system every three to five years. This movement should include records and their associated metadata (a system that generates information about the records).

It is true that the use of electronic records and system has continuously changed the way in which records are generated and managed. In essence electronic records bring fundamental challenges to governmental organisations that create them and make transfer to the archive. However, this does not alter the fact that records need to be managed well and to maintain their integrity and ability to provide evidence. There is a need for this to occur for accountability purposes, to support administrative action, to support recovery after disasters and to foster institutional and social memory. In concordance with the above discussions there are some problems connected with the management of electronic records with some solutions, based on the perceptions of records management practitioners and archivists. It is the responsibility of the electronic records manager of finding ways and means of these problems. In this regard, records and information practitioners caring for records in electronic form about the management and organisational issues would be a relief. Also, issues relating to storage media and some legal issues which include the preparation of records to be admissible in the court of law are all vital solutions.

It is a truism that electronic records are absolutely depended not only on hardware and software systems. But the complication is this system often become obsolete. Thus it has frequently been recognised that complication rarely exists in managing electronic records. In this light, it is argued that there are often challenges in the management of records in other to attain it use and disposability. In this case certain activities in designing electronic records system include:
   a) analysing organisational needs leading to project scoping;
   b) defining systems requirement;
   c) carrying out a benefit analysis;
   d) designing the system;
   e) specification of software requirements;
   f) designing the system architecture;
   g) integrating and testing software;
   h) integrating and testing the system within the organisation framework;
   i) implementing the system; and
   j) maintaining the system(p.22).

4. REGULATORY FRAMEWORK OF ELECTRONIC RECORDS MANAGEMENT

Electronic records management has led to the adoption of new techniques in the governance and public administration that records managers have to struggle with in this 21stcentury. The Electronic Commission and Transaction Act 25(ECT, 2002) was initiated by the South African Government in 1999 to establish a formal structure to define, develop, regulate, and govern e-commerce in South Africa due to the challenges involved in managing electronic records. The ECT is absolutely the most significant piece of legislation ratified in the context of information revolution. One major issue addressed by the Act to records managers in South Africa specially, is to provide for the legal recognition of electronic transactions document and signatory and facilitating records retention electronic evidence and automated transaction. Chapter three of the Act reflects on legal recognition of electronic documents and states that there must be no indifferences of treatment between electronic and paper records. Provision should be made for the recognition of electronic versions of paper based concept and that subject to certain conditions, electronic data will be allowed to be retaining for document retention purposes regarded as original documents. Also, provision should be made for proper securing of electronic evidence in order to acknowledge electronic documents.

With the enacting of ECT Act, 2002, the private sector has shown interest in the discipline of records management, as the realisation of electronic system has now carried the same status in the arena of the law as hardcopy records. These days private sector is embarking on formal records management programme in order to ensure the integrity of electronic records carried in a court of law. In fact in South Africa, it seems that private sector was largely instrumental in securing records management standard. As the ECT Act(2002) accorded equal status to electronic records neglecting to implement formal records management programme for both the sectors, private and publics, can cause a very serious and ever-lasting aftermath. In this case, it must be noted that all electronic records management programme that may be tedious to demonstrate, have compliance with ECT Act and legislative reference.

As the public sector in South Africa has well established a tradition of hard copy records management based programme, it is different for the management of electronic records. However, there are some guidelines for the management of electronic records in the public records from the National Archives of South Africa, and a lot of governmental bodies have implemented electronic management systems, but majority of electronic records are yet to be managed in terms of records management principles in these institutions. Thus before this time the results from the legal perspective were slightly minor. The emergent and implementation of new technology and their growing adoption and use in records and archives institutions are gradually changing the way organisation work, make decision, communicate, and even document their activities. As a result of this, records practitioners should pay attention to records in electronic format.

Unless electronic records are managed better than paper records there will be a steady loss of records and access to the remaining ones. This, will result in making ad hoc decision by management. In addition to that, these things can only occur when paper records, keeping systems are badly managed, but this can happen more frequently and acutely with electronic records. It has been an acceptable generalization that an organisation should develop a strategic framework, policy, and procedures for the management of information. This is true because, the principle and skills acquired by records managers in managing paper records can as well be applied to electronic records. On the other hand, the basic framework about the concept of the life cycle of records management has been accorded and applied to electronic records, but it needs some readjustment in interpretation. Its management should be shifted from physical to intellectual control. Early records managers manage the message by managing the medium. With the advent of electronic records, both are now managed, that is the records content and the physical form. Apparently, managing the medium alone will not help in the management of electronic records. In order to exercise good intellectual control, it is advisable to start managing electronic records as soon as they are created. Otherwise it should be realised that most features of routine records management activities are taken later in the life cycle. With electronic records, the management system should be in place at the beginning, before a record is created.

In most countries new information technologies has changed the way state agencies create, use, disseminate and store information. The legal authority, divisional responsibility, principle of best practices related to electronic recordkeeping by the state agencies are as follows:
- a) government records are public property which cannot be destroyed without authorization from the approved record retention and disposition schedule;
- b) government records are to be kept open for public inspection if it is specifically exempted.

From the aforementioned legislative requirements one can attest that these two Laws provide a potent incentive for agencies to actively engage in electronic records management. One can also argue that state agencies are legally obligated not only to retain all of the electronic records they create also provide public access to them. In this case registered book should be regularly maintained describing both electronic records held by the agency and the form in which they can be made available to the public. Thus the following information should be at least scheduled as follows:
- a) records series titles and description;
- b) minimum retention period;
- c) access requirement and restrictions; and
- d) final disposition requirements (p.3).

Cooperation among management staff within agencies, which create and handle electronic records, information specialist system design, and record officers, is also significant for the management of electronic records. The management of electronic records is a collective responsibility that demands new partnership with state agencies. It must be reckoned that the ability to maintain electronic records and ensure their accessibility over time highly hinges on the way records are created, organised, and maintained in the agencies that create them. Thus individual agencies are most likely to understand their electronic records system and the specific applications required to maintain the records they created. As technology transforms over time, agencies are in the best position to ensure that records of enduring value are successfully transferred as system changes. The following aspects of electronic records keeping under the responsibility of agencies are as follows:

a) the creation and maintenance of reliable and accurate electronic record;
b) ensure that recordkeeping policies and procedures are developed and implemented as part of overall business process;
c) maintenance of electronic record register; and
d) submission of retention and disposition schedules for approval.

The responsibilities of state archives with regard to electronic records management and preservation, it will be difficult to assume these responsibilities given the staffing and level of expertise needed. The principles and best practices of electronic recordkeeping practices is that:

a) agencies should maintain a regular accessibility of records throughout their period of retention;
b) agencies should take measures to ensure the accurate and consistent application of retention schedule to their electronic records;
c) Electronic recordkeeping system should be based on practical open standards;
d) agencies must develop the access to their records in a manner that ensure public access right while also protecting confidentiality;
e) recordkeeping should be addressed in the system planning and development stage rather than waiting until the end of the records life cycle; and
f) agencies should take measures to ensure the reliability and authenticity of records throughout their retention period(p.35).

5. GUIDELINES, POLICIES, PROCEDURES FOR ELECTRONIC RECORDS

Guidelines for managing electronic records should be developed to provide for the retention and disposition of all electronic records, which include those recorded on mainframe, mainframe computer and most recently the websites of states and federal agencies . The National Archives in the UK has published two sets of functional guidelines to promote the development of electronic records management software market (1999-2002). It has run a programme to evaluate products against the 2002 requirements. While these requirements were initially formulated in collaboration with the central government, they have been taken up with enthusiasm by many parts of the wider public sector in the UK and in other parts of the world. However, the most up-to-date guidelines are the MoReq2, published in February 2008 by the European Commission. The two authors argued for the principles/guidelines associated with the developments of records retention schedules for hardcopy and microfilm media; and recognize the most carefully considered operational situation within which records management programme to be implemented as the most potent principles/guidelines to take cognizance of when dealing with electronic records. They also advanced that in creating electronic records such as website, records managers could also think of creating systemic management. This system must be in uniformity with the best operating practices of records management. Thus, in order to set up an electronic records management programme, records manager's most important priority is to conduct a records survey and then adhere to the guidelines highlighted above. The authors concluded that most of the states and federal agencies in the United States of America and UK do not manage websites records according to the records management guidelines stated above which the researcher failed to subscribe to, it is only few unlike Africa.

The formulation of policies that gears towards electronic records should be a broader strategy that links the varied phases of information and communication. In this broader context, it is critical to understand the evidential nature of records, especially electronic records. However, their four main issues are:

a) electronic records have been catalysts for the overall notion that design of records keeping system and defining what they should capture need to be addressed if important records of government are to survive. Thus, techniques to identifying which records have short and long term value will need to change;

b) the management of electronic records requires standards and advice from state records. It should be ensured that agencies be obligatory in authorizing proper disposal. The platform on which electronic records is created requires agencies themselves to ensure that records are transited across systems which ensure the quality of records as evidence is instantly kept;

c) the principal repository for official records is a state records which is no longer required for current administrative purposes, in which case compulsory custody is often transferred from agencies after fifteen(15) years. Electronic records need to have a permanent physical preservation just as paper records. Thus, it is left with the person who can manage, store sort records effectively which should be addressed; and

d) electronic records enable online access and do not require public reading room visit. This creates an environment which ensures the integrity of records, the security of other records, protection of personal privacy other inappropriate disclosures and the respective role of agencies creating records and state records. In this scenario South Australia Government electronic records performance and functions are a key component. Thus sorted records should be prudently managed(p.222).

These days other electronic data that are now commonly created, such as spreadsheets, databases and Power Point presentation pose different and often formidable problems when it comes to incorporating them into paper files. Thus, Montana ardently contended that anyone dealing with records in electronic media should obtain a copy of all relevant guidelines issued by records professional bodies. Despite the possibility of artificial/human interference in the distortion of electronically recorded information, there is also unplanned natural disaster interference. Consequently, there need to be a disaster recovery control plan to be initiated by the records manager in collaboration with other personnel in the organisation. The point must be strictly highlighted that even in a small electronic records environment, creators of electronic records will be required to acquire records management skills. And such skills will be required to make records management decisions which include the development of written policies and procedures in all but a small environment.

Thus implementation of a short set of procedures, combined with a standard indexing system and a naming and versioning convention for documents, will yield surprisingly good results. In general, these policies and procedures will consist of one or more of the following: a Records and Information(RIM) policy, including policies for drafts, duplicates and transient records; a records retention schedule; a standard data structure or indexing scheme; a naming and versioning convention for records sets; and procedures that indicate the way the above should be instructed as the principle do not change over time while the conceptual tools change only gradually, if at all. And there should be well organised records management workshops to sensitize records staff, administrators, and other real creators of electronic information on the way these records should be managed and the challenges they must address in order to manage electronic records most effectively. In this light, it is good to consider electronic records management based on the experience of other countries' governmental issues.

The existence of a policy serves as a guideline to facilitate actions and decisions to be taken. It is noted that advances in Information and Communication Technology(ICT) provide the opportunity for governments to improve their delivery of information and services to citizens, and businesses to streamline public sector functions, and to increase participation in government. This is just a matter of providing electronic access to information in some countries. In reality, electronic services, such as land searches or submission of tax revenue, are being delivered online. They asserted that electronic government has the potential to mitigate constraints imposed by distance and increase the speed of service delivery. However it also poses a number of challenges for accountability, the rule of law and the maintenance of organisational memory. Thus, the only way to overcome the challenges is to provide electronic management guidelines that are clear, comprehensive, and understandable to direct the organisation and ascertain the effectiveness of functions implemented. The purpose of the study was to investigate whether government agencies in Malaysia do poses such a policy guidelines for electronic records management. The survey employed a questionnaire to gather the data for twenty-five (25) selected government departments in Klang Valley and Putrajaya, Malaysia. The findings from the administered questionnaires revealed that not all governments possessed electronic records management policies that are clear, complete and easy to implement. Thus organisations are using policy provided by Malaysian Administrative Modernisation and Management Planning Unit (MAMPU) and the National Archives of Malaysia (NAM) with some modifications to suit their needs. On the other hand, the number of organisations carrying out electronic records management without any policy in place is alarming. In this vein, electronic records management carried out in some organisations are merely based on their instinct and initiatives, far from complying with international standards of best practice. Thus the researcher of this study has used this method to carry out the investigation in the use of electronic records management guidelines to manage electronic records at Ministry of Finance and Economic Development (MoFED), Sierra Leone. However, the only problem with this method is that there was no testing of hypothesis in order to confirm the validity of the result.

The Kansas Records Management Guidelines involved in establishing a policy framework for implementing sound electronic records keeping practice as a whole as essential in public service. Good electronic records keeping will reduce the cost of government, improve the delivery of services and support accountability. It furthered that this gain could only be possible if a sound policy framework for electronic records keeping is established. This policy should relate to electronic records keeping in general with principles which public sector institutions should incorporate into their records keeping strategies and initiatives to ensure the effective management of electronic records. These principles should include electronic records keeping being incorporated into records management programme by the public sector, through the development and implementation of policies, procedures and systems. Thus, electronic records keeping should become a routine occurrence of business in the electronic environment by building it into business processes and tools and using existing infrastructure more effectively.

Further there is a number of mechanisms which need to be developed in order to assist the public sector in implementing the policies, guidelines and related standards in electronic records keeping. It considered the following:

a) desktop management: which deals with guidelines for managing electronic documents and directories that enhance the minimisation of threats to loss of unmanaged electronic records that may be on personal computer system in a short while;
b) records keeping system design: this entails developing manuals to give practical guidance to institutions for the design and implementation of records keeping system;
c) records management software utilisation: this involves the assurance of organisations to approve records management software products to facilitate electronic records keeping;
d) training and education: this includes all policies, standards, codes of best practice and guidelines about training and education conducted for stakeholders and records keeping practitioners.

Business conducted in electronic environments should be documented properly to meet the requirements of operational and community accountability. This entails making and keeping records in an electronic system to advance the use of machine learning for the automation of records classification and disposal systems. Indeed there are already commercial records management products available that use machine learning such as auto-classification, to improve search. Generally it has been debated that improved electronic records keeping is significant to the success of government's goal for information management and technology. The policy document outlines principles which agencies should stick by in developing practices and system for recordkeeping in an electronic environment. Thus the State Archives and Records of New South Wales major policies for the management of electronic records are explained below:

a) Electronic records created or received by an agency or government employees in the course of official duties are to be treated as official records. As records of government or agencies, electronic records, like in other format, are subject to laws such as Freedom of Information Act and legal processes. These records may be required by Commissions, Courts and Auditors. In essence electronic records keeping should comply with recognised best practice in the electronic environment as in the paper environment. Also, electronic records keeping should be built into business processed and tools. That is recordkeeping should be a daily routine of business entities in the electronic environment.

b) Any business conducted by electronic means should be adequately documented to meet standard records keeping requirements. This means that agencies should ensure that they adequately and appropriately document those activities of their business that are written in the record. These records should satisfy identified business needs, accountability and community expectations.

c) Electronic records keeping should be maintained in a reliable records keeping system. This implies that agencies should engage in systematic electronic records keeping practices via the design and operation of reliable electronic recordkeeping system. In this case one can argue that reliable records keeping produce authentic and trustworthy records. This principle requires that agencies establish policies, rules, formats, methodologies and procedures incorporating sound records keeping practices. Thus all electronic recordkeeping by agencies need to be documented and assign responsibilities regarding modification on their development operation and use.

d) As part of comprehensive records management programme, electronic records should be managed effectively. In essence, agencies should ensure that policies and practices for management of digital records are entirely incorporated into general record management programmes. It must be reckoned that electronic record and paper records document the same business activities; and agencies concerned should manage these records in such a way that is clear, accessible and easily retrieved. To realize this accessibility, it must be a shared responsibility between agencies and the archives.

However, the policy document of State Archive and Records of New South Wales has made tremendous improvement across NSW government, and organisations in transforming from desktop application and migrating their emails, document storage, project management, collaboration and other business software to software-as-a-service platform like Microsoft Office 365. Some organisations have started using this product, but records professional in these organisations are amongst the least to find out. Thus 'digital transformation' is a priority of NSW Government, Transitioning from manual and paper-based processes to automated and digitally enabled processes is expected to simplify and streamline the work of government, as digital transactions and processes are generally faster, more convenient and more efficient. Digital transformation also creates information risk.

6. IT SPECIALIST AND RECORDS MANAGER

To gain a transparent picture of electronic records, there is no better frontier than Information Technology (IT) specialists and their close friends. There should be a reciprocal interaction between a software specialist and a records manager and this needs to be initiated at the commencement of any records management project so as to permit computer based management of electronic records be set up at the design stage. A life cycle principle of appraising records is very important

especially when it comes to the management control of electronic media. Thus information professionals must be aware of this basic caveat for the management of records, no matter the media. And with electronic records there is a great need for intellectual control of records. Answers to the following points will be elicited provided the environment within which the information is created used, maintained and disposed of, established, and the basic tenets for the control of the medium explored:
- a) What types of records need to be controlled; how are they used currently and by whom?
- b) Who need access to them and why?
- c) Where are they sent and how?
- d) How are they modified?
- e) Are there any trials for modification?
- f) What is the duration for keeping them? And does the medium need changing for retention purposes?

Form the aforementioned questions; one can gain an explorative awareness in the issue of controlling electronic medium. This can start from the basic fact of flexibility in the use of electronic records which is not apparent with the hard copy form and this indicates some challenges for some who handle records in this format. The legality of recorded information and accessibility of that information has to be addressed via the whole life cycle of information. Thus, there is nothing to be baffled with if one cannot manage information in any medium of the present, one cannot manage it neither in the future. Records practitioners need to adopt a sensible and laudable approach to managing electronically recorded information with the same professionalism as their predecessors have always been doing. Frankly, one can contend that the management of electronic records is renowned. The often but neglected basic point to consider when thinking of retention of electronic media is that of reading electronic record at later date, one needs not only to be able to recall the recorded information but also have the hardware needed to play it back. It should be noted that it is the content of the information than the form which the records manager is concerned with; it can be a difficult task to identify what the content of an electronic document is. Thus it is worth contemplating about applying the principles of centralised records management. In dealing with electronic records consistent standards have to be applied and defined for future reference guidelines.

It has been over a hundred years when information specialists tried to device a way in the modification of their process for records and archives administration. This modification is the records and transition to digital system in managing the creation, use, preservation and disposal of electronic information in context. Tough further argued that these days information specialists are being forced to re-evaluate/transit everything practically possible as they are faced with serious challenges posed by managing the growing number of electronic records. In this light, a piece of advice was offered in dealing with a lot of conceptual and operational issues for the management of electronic records. And it matters most if records managers, archivists, and other information management professionals responsible for the retention, storage, and protection of electronic document to take the following into cognizance:

a) the significance of electronic records as business information resources;
b) special problems associated with electronic records and the key components;
c) step by step programme to manage them;
d) inventoried;
e) making retention decisions;
f) stability of electronic records; and
g) storage system(p.20).

Electronic records management the greatest professional challenge to archivist and records managers in developing countries, especially in sub- Sahara Africa since the 1990s. Electronic records possess certain challenges and implication, particularly the appraisal of electronic records to archivists. Thus with the development of computers, records are generated in electronic format. With regards to the management of such records, a number of professionals, managerial and technical issues are aroused or expected to arise. Professional issues will often infringe on decision on the creation, storage access, use, appraisal, retention and disposition. It should be noted that technical issues will basically focus on the selection of hardware and software, maintenance system, upgrading and training system. The managerial issues will deal with information technology policy, training of staff and resource sharing. These issues demand various forms of sensitization and awareness training of the existing records management staff in order to make them understand their changing responsibility in a dynamic information environment. This key enabler of electronic records needs to be considered in order to establish effective electronic management programme. In this case, electronic records are easily manipulated and overwritten; once the database is created and networked such security measures should be needed to prevent an unauthorised access to such records particularly financial records. In this scenario, the creator of records has to be involved in the appraisal decision making. This should happen as early as possible regarding the necessity of creating certain records and the timeframe of the retention and disposition schedule so as to determine the action to be taken on electronic records based on records functionality and there is need to determine the standard of archival versions of electronic records. The researcher is in support of the above view, if and only if records management skills are transferred to creators of electronic information so that this can affect the appraising and disposition decision. Today, the lack of Information Technology (IT) skills and professional knowhow in the training of records management pose severe problems such as poorly organised paper system for records, inadequate records management skills amongst registry staff and the absence of a records management policy to address issues gearing to the management of both paper and electronic records. In conclusion, record personnel need to be conversant with records management practices and techniques which they must try to impart to creators in an electronic environment.

7. IMPORTANCE OF KEEPING ELECTRONIC RECORDS

The benefit electronic record can bring huge benefit provided there is an appropriate infrastructure to support it, and this includes adequate provisions to manage and protect the records generated. It is significant that everyone concerned should recognize that computer generates records and that keeping these records needs greater discipline than keeping paper records:

a) it will provide a facelift to records and archival institutions and will allow interactions in such jobs like acquisition or creation, filling system, security control, appraisal, retention and storage system;

b) It will also allow the use of reference database on CD-ROM, diskette and tapes used by the records management institutions;

c) It will help in the handling of records and in maintaining accurate and up-to-date files, with little staff involvement;

d) It will economise records staff's resources, avert duplication of work, and thus lead to improved control of records operation and management;

e) It will facilitate resource sharing and dissemination of information; and

f) It will lead to a reduction of cost in electronic records management operations(p.200).

The researcher is in support of Asamoah's view but only when certain basic requirements are considered namely:

a) appropriate provision in legislation both for the management of electronic records and for legal admissibility;

b) well-organised, accurate, and easily accessible source data;

c) appropriate system design, including provision for capture of contextual data and realistic targets;

d) clearly defined backup and storage procedures;

e) appropriate environmental conditions and physical security; and

f) sufficient budget allocations to cover all cost.

Electronic computing has become the most important instrument because of its power to transform the way people work. This is due to the fact that the wide spread use of computers has been the most vital technique to affect the field of records management. Since computers produce fabulous quantities of records for records staff to manage, there are enormous problems connected with the management of electronic records; problems that demand records management solutions as computers provide a lot of tools for the solution of management problems. But records managers should note that all electronic records maintained on removable electronic media be labeled, identified, and catalogued in such a way that enhances effective management. Thus, a variety of software available enable the management of electronic records that rely on standalone personal computers (PCs), as well as those connected to networks.

Conclusively, it must be noted that both financial and no-financial records management should be integrated into electronic records management systems within agencies which requires a diverse approach. In this case Ministries, Agencies and Departments should effectively utilize available expertise in the institutions or elsewhere because there would be some staff that are responsible for paper record whiles the others for electronic records. This expertise includes records management, both paper and electronic records keeping; Information management and technology; business system analysis and design risk assessment; auditing; and the law respectively. It is believed that the challenges of capturing and managing both paper and electronic records have compelled records managers and archivist to revisit their prestigious professional career.

On this note incorporating records keeping requirements into electronic system is very critical to business processes especially financial management public sector business processes and their compliances regime, on which records are documented on their activities; for short, medium and long term business, legal, social and cultural information, and accountability purposes in enhancing good governance. Again, the foregoing information about the activities of business entities' data, content, structure and context should be properly captured and maintained for enhancing good governance in a public sector. The too much use of literature in developed countries is a clear manifestation of the dearth of published literature on records management in developing countries which illustrate the gap in relevant literature that justified the need for this study.

PART 4:
SURVEY APPROACH TO RECORDS MANAGEMENT

1. INTRODUCTION

This part deals with the design of the study. It deals with research variables, population studied, research samples, research instruments, method of collecting data, method of analyzing data, ethical considerations and constraints. These issues are the barometer which the analysis of data hinges on.

2. RESEARCH VARIABLES

Research variables are those aspects of the study that can be interpreted by using descriptive statistics. A variable is a representative of any outcome or characteristics that may change in quantity and/or quality in the course of carrying out the study. These outcomes could be dependent and independent variables. A dependent variable is the specific outcome or condition while the independent variable is that which explains the causes of the dependent variable. For example, implementing records management policies, guidelines and procedures enhances accountability and transparency (good governance) in the management of records at Ministry of Finance and Economic Development (MoFED). In this case 'policy' is an independent variable while 'governance' is a dependent variable.

In quantitative studies for example, researchers use quantitative research questions and hypotheses, and sometimes objectives, to specifically shape and focus on the main purpose and objectives of the study. Quantitative research questions inquest about the relationships among variables that researchers seek to know. Quantitative hypotheses on the other hand, are predictions of an expected relationship among variables. However, in this survey, the research variables that are interpreted statistically based on the questionnaires administered are records; policies; official correspondences, workshop documents and reports;

rules and regulations framework; standards and guidelines for records management; equipment and supplies; and users.

3. POPULATION STUDIED

Whether the researcher is engaged in experimental or non-experimental research, the actual study is conducted on a sample drawn from the population of interest. "Population" is defined as a larger group on which one intends to conduct a survey. "Population" is a collection of items of interest in a statistical study. And "Population" is defined as a total number of all the people (or animals, places, objects, events) on which the research is conducted. In this research the population studied totaled one hundred and three (103) staff of MoFED registry/administration. These were divided into fifty (50) civil servant officers, forty (40) contract officers, and thirteen (13) other staff, about whom the researcher made generalisation because they were linked to all the other units within the MoFED institution.

4. RESEARCH SAMPLE

A research sample is a selection of items (including people, institutions) from a population to give information about that population. There are varied types of sampling techniques used by researchers which include the following:
  a) Simple random sampling-This deals with the selection of participants each of whom has an equal chance of being selected. It is also called a probabilistic sampling;
  b) Systematic sampling-This is a sample obtained by picking participants at random from the first participant and every deciding participants thereafter until the total number of participants is obtained;
  c) Quota sampling- This is a set of number or quota of subjects with specific outcomes;
  d) Stratified sampling-This is a random sample obtained by picking a simple random sample in each of the strata. The drawing of the samples is carried out independently in different stratum. Also, a number of participants picked in a stratum may vary from stratum to stratum. However, a proportional allocation method is used for

obtaining a sample size in each stratum proportional to the size of stratum. This means that the more the population the higher the sample chosen and the lesser the population the lesser the sample chosen to form a stratum and each stratum is proportional to each other.

Random sampling suggests the way one can be confident in generalizing from a sample to a population of interest. This connotes that instead of using any characteristics to decide which ones are in the sample, a variable is used whose values are randomly determined. However, qualitative researchers are identified with non-random or purposeful sampling while quantitative researchers are identified with random sampling. This research study used stratified random samples. The rationale for using this method is to increase precision/accuracy of participants because the variability within each stratum is reduced due to internal homogeneity. Also, by dividing the population into strata and picking a sample from each stratum, it is evident that each sub-population is adequately represented. Subjects were deliberately selected, because these are the staff who acts on mandate to ensuring sound records management practice at MoFED Registry/Administration in enhancing good governance.

This study also basically focused on staff with the mandate of implementing and managing MoFED Registry/Administration records that have a relationship with National Records Centre and the Public Archives Office, Sierra Leone. It must be recognised as it is impossible to interview every individual beneficiary; stratified random sampling was used to get a sample of participants. The participant of the study has been stratified into: twenty-five (25) Civil Servant Officers (CSOs), twenty (20) Contract Officers (COs) and fifteen(15) others respectively involved in the creation, receipts and management of records. The list of the aforementioned categories of staff of MoFED serves as a sample size comprising sixty participants being interviewed as informants. They are presumed to be conversant with issues bordering effective records management. It must be highlighted that members of these groups were randomly selected. Like any other sample population, it is expected that after the sampling, the information obtained from the sample population will be true of the parent population. In essence random sampling serves not only to equate two or more experimental groups but to make whatever group one's study makes representative of the larger population. It is also a fair procedure whereby all subjects in a given population have equal chance of being included in the study. Random sampling enhances the selected sample to be true of the larger population. It increases the external validity of research. Thus the responses from participants to the questionnaire were used to draw conclusions relating to the research objectives. It further outlines the rate of responses from participants which is further explained in part five.

5. RESEARCH INSTRUMENT

Research instrument is a tool used in collecting data from a field study and it provides a reliable method for analysis. For example, ranking, pair-wise ranking, circular or Venn diagrams, observation, interview, and questionnaire are all research instruments. However, few of these tools are used as discussed below.

An interview is defined as a process in which a researcher and a participant engage in a conversation focused on a question related to the study. An interview is engaged to understand people, perceptions, opinions, feelings and thoughts. Interviews are classified according to the amount of structure that they carry. The classes are highly structured, semi-structured and unstructured. In highly structured interviews, questions and the order which they are asked are determined ahead of time. A highly structured interview could be problematic in this research because rigidly adhering to predetermined questions may not allow the researcher to access participant's perceptions and understandings of the world. Instead one get reactions to the investigator preconceived notions of such a world.

Questionnaires are regarded as essential research instruments. Questionnaire is defined as the careful list of questions designed to obtain information for research study. And data are generally collected using a standardised questionnaire, which may be administered in a face-to-face interview or as a self-administered questionnaire. However, the process of developing a well-standardised and user-friendly instrument for collecting data is complex and time consuming, but crucial for successful research. Convincingly, the questionnaire method used as a research instrument is an effective way of obtaining data about people and cannot be challenged. This means that data about people via direct questions is crucial, because its authority is more likely to be authoritatively accurate than employing the method of observation. Moreover, questionnaires are easily administered especially when the researcher comes in contact with participants personally, by phone, by email or by computer. Reliable questionnaires yield consistent results from repeated samples and from different researchers' over a given period of time. Differences in results come from differences between participants, not from inconsistencies as to how the items are understood or how different observers interpret the responses. A standardised questionnaire is one that is written and administered wherein all participants are asked precisely similar questions in an identical format and responses recorded in a uniform manner. Standardising a measure is a means of increasing reliability.

A questionnaire was used as main instrument in collecting data for this study at MoFED registry/administration in Sierra Leone. The questionnaire was pilot-tested to ten(10) administrative staff at MoFED for clarity, ease of use and to avoid duplicity of questions. One major challenge the author experienced with this exercise was that some of the questions contained in the questionnaire were blurred while some were too long to be easily understood by participants. The other challenge was that the terminology used was confusing. It should be noted that these questionnaires were refined and divided into sections.

The questionnaire to MoFED Registry/administration staff was designed after fruitful discussion with representative samples of the foregoing staff of the Ministry. The questionnaire for use sought information from MoFED staff concerning the management of records in enhancing good governance at MoFED Registry/Administration to be specific. The questionnaire had both structured/close-ended (using the Likert scales) and unstructured/open-ended questions. The rationale for using both close and open-ended questions was due to flexibility; and it allowed the researcher to delve into the subject at greater depth since open-ended questions can be time-consuming to administer and analyse results which warranted the researcher/author to use close ended questions. Because of this, piloting and formative research was conducted in order to facilitate the use of open ended questions which provided suggestions for standard responses that was pre-coded and included in the questionnaire. The refined questionnaire sought information on the following:

a) Personal information;
b) Types of records generated;
c) Legal and regulatory framework;
d) Standard, codes, policies and procedures;
e) Facilities, equipment, and supplies;
f) Monitoring and compliance with phases of records keeping;
g) Disposition and retention procedures;
h) Users' security and training;
i) Information Communication Technology(ICT); and
j) Good governance, transparency and accountability at MoFED.

Other instruments used to complement the questionnaire were observation of MoFED staff at work and examination of the documentation of the system. The observation method was chosen because it was at the convenience of participants, who for the success of this study were of great importance that needed to be satisfied in order to not only increase their response rate but also the reliability of the research study.

6. METHOD OF COLLECTING DATA

Before the research began in earnest, a pilot study was conducted with MoFED staff on 10th January, 2018. Three people were interviewed, to obtain an understanding of the current state of functioning in the MoFED concerning the objective of the study. Each interview lasted twenty(20) minutes, and served to establish relationships with MoFED staff and to clarify questions and unclear answers on the questionnaires administered. The main data were collected on diverse dates between the months of February and March 2018.

Prior to data collection exercise, a formal letter of introduction was sent to the MoFED registry/ administration unit staff for a period of one week. The researcher used primary and secondary data sources as a means of gathering data. Data is defined as nothing more than ordinary bits and pieces of information found in the environment .There are two types of data namely primary data and secondary data. Primary data refer to a situation where there has been no data collection earlier from an enquiry. Such data are called fresh/original data. This is relatively error-free and hence more accurate, although time-consuming and costly. Secondary data on the other hand refer to those that have been collected earlier on and normally for different purposes than what the current research intends to achieve. It could be both published and unpublished data and normally subjected to printing errors but less time consuming and less costly to collect. Virtually, the primary data have been collected from participants asking questions arising from the semi-structured personal interviews, self-administered questionnaire, telephoning and emailing methods used. However, the researcher administered sixty questionnaires of which 50(83.3%) were returned in usable form while 10(16.7%) were not returned from the aforementioned categories of staff to complement the study in question. The secondary data were collected from papers presented in conference proceedings, workshops, and seminars, reports by MoFED, the Sierra Leone Government, and articles from online journals.

7. METHOD OF ANALYSING DATA

Data analysis is the process of making sense of data. And making sense of data involves consolidating, reducing, and interpreting what people have said and what the researcher has read; it is the process of making meaning to the collected data. Basically data analysis is the process that is used to answer the research question(s) from the collected data. Qualitative data analysis consists of three concurrent flow of activities:

data reduction, data display and conclusion drawing or verification and are emergent, which means that analysis are revolved as the research develops. Collection and analysis of data are done simultaneously. On the other hand, quantitative analysis involves transforming endless pages of words, numbers, and codes into meaningful result to informed theory building or action. However one of the common limitations of survey research is the tendency to present results mostly in the form of descriptive statistics, that is, percentages.

The researcher/author gathered data to build concepts, hypotheses or theories from bits and pieces of information from interviews, questionnaires and documents and these were combined and scored into frequencies and percentages; pie and bar charts were extrapolated as the researcher worked from particular experiences of MoFED staff to general conclusions and recommendations. Quantitative researchers seek explanations and make predictions that will generalize to other persons and places. In this research the triangulation method was used because the researcher /author wished to understand the particular depth of the challenges faced by MoFED staff in pursuing their mandate and what the reasons behind the current state in the management of its records.

The researcher utilised qualitative analysis in the reduction, display and verification of data for in-depth analysis; while the use of quantitative analysis enabled the researcher to compute response using Microsoft Excel (2010) and Statistical Package for Social Sciences Version Sixteen(SPSS 16.0) and extrapolated charts as these enhanced a reliable and trustworthy outcome of the research process .

The researcher also used Z-score and probability value to test the varied variables with a stipulated 5% significance level of α(alpha). In Statistics, a Z-score is signed standard number of standard deviation by which the value of an observation or data point is above the mean value of what is being observed or measured. Observed values above the mean/average participants have positive standard scores, while values below the mean have negative standard scores. On the other hand, standard score is the dimensionless quantity obtained by subtracting the population mean from an individual raw score/datum and then dividing the difference by the population standard deviation; and a P-value is obtained from a statistical table corresponding to Z-score value(Free encyclopaedia, 2018). Thus the computation of Z-score was done via the use of (SPSS 16.0) which codes/data points ranging from 1-8 and others 1-3 were inputted into it, based on the number of samples collected. The researcher then selected the least frequency of Z-score value to represent the variables stated in part six.

8. ETHICAL CONSIDERATIONS

Ethical considerations in research are critical. Ethics are the norms or standards for conduct that distinguish between right and wrong. They help to determine the differences between acceptable and unacceptable behaviours. Ethical considerations are important for varied reasons. Foremost, ethical standards prevent the fabrication or falsifying of data and therefore, promote the pursuit of knowledge and truth which is the primary goal of research. Ethical behaviour is also critical for collaborative work because it encourages an environment of trust, accountability, and mutual respect among researchers. Because ethical considerations are so crucial in research, many agencies and professional institutions such as Fourah Bay College, University of Sierra Leone, have adopted codes and policies that outlined ethical behaviour and guides to researchers. These codes and policies address issues such as anonymity, confidentiality, observation of rights, protection of data/respect for intellectual property, acknowledging authors of sources used, objectivity, obliging a fair copy to the case study, honesty, social responsibility, non-discrimination and many others. These codes and policies provide basic guidelines, but researchers will still be faced with additional issues that are not specifically addressed and this will require decision-making on the part of the researcher in order to avoid misconduct.

For purpose of this research, the researcher made the conditions of anonymity very clear to participants. This included not revealing their names in the research, but just mentioning their designation and category of staff they belonged. To this, participants agreed and only the information given was used to make presentation and analysis as the names of participants were not an issue in this case. No one other than the researcher knew who provided the information. However, some participants said they were not concerned if their names were used as this was not going to jeopardise them in any way.

In terms of confidentiality the researcher assured participants in advance that their information would be handled confidentially and not disclosed outside the realm of this research. This helped to put participants at ease when responding to the questionnaires.

The right of participants was also observed in order not to violate their human rights in anyway as they were told that there was no harm in the form of stress, pain, anxiety, diminishing self-esteem or/and evasion of privacy in participation which may cause human rights abuse.

The protection of raw data was another ethical consideration which the researcher took into cognizance by coding them using the Statistical Package for Social Sciences (SPSS 16.0) for security purpose which cannot be understood by anybody other than the researcher till the final copy was published for research purpose. Also, the researcher acknowledged the authors of sources used by way of referencing.

For any research to be successful there must be credibility and trust, experience, good track record, status and presentation of self. Honesty must prevail in research work as plagiarism is a gross manifestation of unethical behaviour which will jeopardise the results of the study. The researcher however avoided plagiarism.

Objectivity in research is an important ethical consideration. Fair treatment was given to participants to ensure that the research report is free from personal bias and opinions. A fair copy was obliged to the MoFED, for ethical reasons as this would portray that the results of the study about the Ministry were accurate and represent what the researcher observed. Thus participants' responses were not taken out of context nor were the discussions from small part of the observation in order to put them in appropriate contexts.

9. CONSTRAINTS

There is no research without constraints. Foremost, there was a problem of choosing the methods of collecting data and analyzing them in order to achieve the ultimate goal of this research. The researcher encountered some constraints during the data collection process. For example, the researcher found it difficult to sit and discuss with senior managers pertinent issues relevant to the study. Participants too needed a thorough explanation of what was on occasion. Some participants failed to follow directives in responding to questions. The high cost of Internet charges and sometimes poor network system which deterred the quick access to online documents was another constraint. Also, there was delay in responding to the questionnaire in the unit in question, and a difficulty in determining who was directly responsible to respond to questions in the MoFED registry/administration. Such predicaments made it difficult for the researcher to determine the accuracy of participants' response in some important areas despite using the triangulation method to achieving accurate response.

In conclusion, the design of the study gives way to part five (5) which deals with data analysis. This includes research variables, population, samples, and instruments, methods of collecting data, method of analysing data, ethical considerations and constraints. All these play a pivotal role in research activities guiding the researcher in carrying out analysis to achieve the ultimate goal of this research.

PART 5:
ANALYSIS AND DISCUSSION

1. INTRODUCTION

This part provides both qualitative and quantitative data derived from varied collection techniques as indicated in the third chapter in this research study. It further focuses on findings via analysing participants' responses to the questionnaire. Data obtained from questionnaires are presented in the form of frequencies (number of participants), percentages, bar and pie charts. Responses were computed using Statistical Packages for Social Sciences (SPSS) and Excel spread sheet 2010 respectively; followed by discussions from interview, observation, reports, books, journal articles and internet. Also, a Z-score and Probability-value was critical towards the testing of the hypothesis stated in chapter one, through the use of variables (independent and dependent variables) in the questionnaire relating to specific objectives of the study. However, fourteen variables (Records Generated (RG), Legal and Regulatory Framework (LRF), Policies, Standards Procedures and Guidelines (PSPG), Facilities, Equipment and Supplies(FES), Monitoring and Compliance (MC), Disposition and Retention Schedule (DRS), Challenges for Managing Records (CMR), Missing, Lost/Damaged Records (MLDR), Qualification/Competencies (Q/C), Training Facilities (TF), Information Communication Technology(ICT), Electronic Records Management Policies (ERMP), MoFED Records/Administration and National Archives (MoFEDR/A&NA) and Good Governance Accountability and Transparency (GGAT)) were statistically tested to prove whether or not sound records keeping enhance good governance at MoFED.

Table 5.0.1: Total number of questionnaires administered

Strata	Questionnaires administered	Questionnaires returned in usable form	Questionnaires not returned
Civil Servant Officers(CSOs)	25(46.7%)	23(46%)	2(3.3%)
Contract Officers(COs)	20(33.3%)	14(28%)	6(10.1%)
Others	15(25%)	13(26%)	2(3.3%)
Total Participants	60 (100%)	50(83%)	10(16.7%)

(Source: Field data on 8th/04/2018 and excel spreadsheet 2010)

Table 5.0.1 shows that out of 60(100%) participants, 25(46.7%) Civil Servant Officers (SCOs), 20(33.3%) Contract Officers (COs) and 15(25%) others were administered questionnaires in stratum. It also shows that 23(46%) of the Civil servant Officers (CSOs), 14(28%) Contract Officers (COs) and 13(26%) Others were returned in usable form while 2(3.3%) Civil Servant Officers (CSOs), 6(10.1%) Contract Officers (Cos) and 2(3.3%) Others were not returned from aforementioned category of staff to complement the study in question.

2. SPECIFIC OBJECTIVES

Specifically the following questions were answered by participants using questionnaire and the researcher computed the data into statistical form:
   a) Which types of records are generated by and received at MoFED? what policies and legislation exist for the management of both financial and non-financial records at MoFED?
   b) Are facilities, equipment and supplies provided for proper management of records? how are records managed in relation to disposition and retention schedule and monitoring at MoFED?

c) Who are the users of records at MoFED and why do they use these records? what competencies/qualification do users and managers possess in managing these records in overcoming challenges faced?
d) Is there an ICT unit at MoFED institution overseeing other units' computer system, and a laid down policy/legal framework for the management of electronic records at MoFED?
e) Does sound records keeping enhance governance, transparency, and accountability at MoFED institution? and is there a relationship between MoFED registry/administration and the National Archives?

Objective(a)-Types of Records Generated, Legislations and Policies, Standard Procedures and Guidelines at MoFED registry/administration.

a. Variable 1-Records Generated (RG)

The variable for this objective depicts the types of records generated or received by MoFED registry/administration in executing its daily functions. Records are information contained in a document detailing the activities of MoFED.

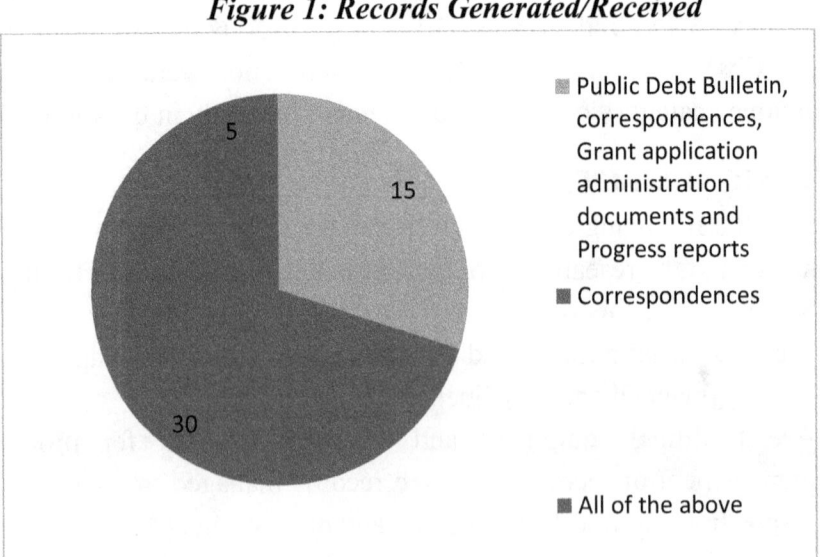

Figure 1: Records Generated/Received

(Source: Field data on 9th/04/2018; SPSS version 16 and excel spreadsheet 2010).

From figure 1 above, (60(f=30)) participants representing the largest portion of red sector indicated that 'correspondences' are some of the materials/records generated/received; (30(f=15)) in the orange sector represents participants' view; and (10(f=5)) in the blue sector of the chart represents some of the participants' view as indicated in the questionnaire are records generated and received by MoFED registry/administration only.

Discussion

Contrary to figure 1, the majority of the records indicated by participants are non-financial. Financial records should be managed in such a way that could enhance transparency by stakeholders who include Accountants and Records Managers. A well-qualified Accountant and Records Manager should be employed to manage financial records. Thus, Records Managers and Accountants should work in tandem as both of them should have proper records knowledge to control cash, as liquidity is the key to the success of public sector organisations. Both financial and records managers play a pivotal role in the decision making process of any organisation. With their experience they are in a greater position to measure financial performance and position of an organisation. From the data collected, it was revealed that the records centre at MoFED registry/administration only held non-financial records as portrayed in the percentage above, that is sixty percent (60%).

As records management is defined as the systematic control of all records from their creation or receipt, via processing, distribution, organisation, storing and retrieval to their ultimate disposition. All organisations generate and manage records be they public or private entities because records are pivotal to enhancing transparency when well-managed. Records can be tangible paper objects or they can be in digital or electronic documents form. These records can be kept on financial, medical, informative, formal documents, office documents, payroll, government forms and emails. This is evidenced in MoFED's administration as it depends more on the proper management of records highlighted in the questionnaire in order to achieve its ultimate goal. Participants were further asked to list the type of records generated that were not included in those listed in the questionnaire. Some participants did state that at MoFED registry/administration, subject files, departmental files which mostly comprise individual/personnel files and ministerial files are received/generated but financial records are not generated or received by them. The reasons given by most participants were that the management of records at MoFED is decentralised. Although financial records are more sensitive documents and should not be duplicated in order to avoid wastages of the scarce resources. Participants were also asked to confirm the cost-effectiveness of the generation/receipt and management of those records and majority consented that the management of records at MoFED is cost-effective. Thus, the cost-effectiveness of records management is all about managing the availability of allocated funds or resources of an organisation such as Ghana during the records management reform programme which brought on board changes in the registries of public sector, new legislative framework was put in place, a functional records centre was restructured, and omnibus retention schedule was reviewed and a number of untrained staff were trained and retrained. Subscribing to this view, even when the funds are available but if not prudently utilized, the listed factors will not be restructured. Thus this is quite different from what MoFED is going through currently.

b. Variable 2-Legal and Regulatory Framework (LRF)
The variable for this objective investigated the legal and regulatory framework for the management of MoFED records for which data collected from participants were computed into frequencies and percentages respectively. This variable indicates the law governing the creation and use of record at MoFED.

Figure 2: Legal and Regulatory Framework

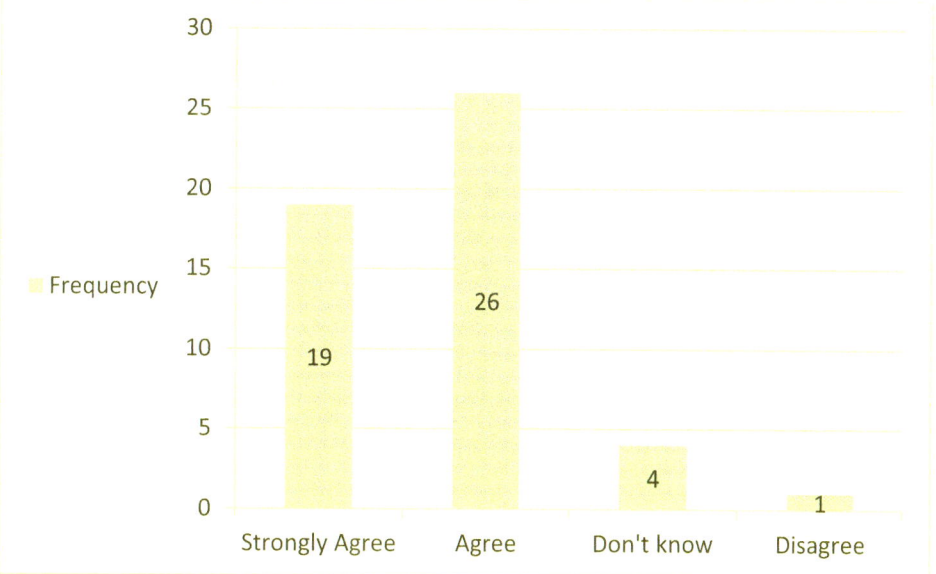

(Source: Field data on 9th/04/2018; SPSS Version 16 and excel spread sheet 2010).

Figure 2 represents participants' degree of agreement as to whether or not there is a primary legislation in place that provides direct guidance on the management of financial and non-financial records at MoFED registry/administration (for e.g. Public Records/National Archive Act). Thirty-eight percent of nineteen(38(f=19)) participants "strongly agreed" that there is a Public Records Act; (52(f=26)) participants "agreed" that public records legislation is available; (8(f=4)) participants were "undecided" that public records legislation is either in place or not in place, while (2(f=1)) participant "disagreed" with the availability of public records legislation at MoFED registry/administration unit for the management of records. And no participant "strongly disagreed" that there is public records legislation.

Discussion

From the figure above, the highest bar reveals that indeed there exists public records legislation at MoFED for the management of records in achieving its ultimate goals. Another sub-question was asked about secondary legislation in place as indirect guidance for the management of financial and non-financial records (e.g the 1991 National Constitution Act, Right to Access Information(RAI) Act, Finance and Audit Act). However, majority of the participants agreed that they are aware of such legislations especially the 1991 National Constitution Act and the RAI Act of 2013 but not effectively and efficiently utilised. And that these laws are not consistent with their requirements for managing records and also are not frequently up-dated due to their importance. Some participants agreed that these laws mandate users to appraise, retain and dispose of public records.

Against this background, archives and records management are based on the records series concept and two primary principles: records life cycle and records appraisal. In this case even legally enforceable right of access to information is meaningless if government records are not in proper order. Even when the information would be available in principle, if it cannot be found then it cannot be made available to their citizens. Thus, this scenario can limit both government's accountability and capacity to discharge its duties with credibility in the eyes of their citizens. Since financial records are found throughout an organisation, their planning, appraisal and implementation of disposal process requires co-operation and co-ordination throughout the organisation to ensure that audit trials and the evidential qualities of records are maintained while the volume of records is controlled. And planning and appraisal of financial records should be contained in the legislations and regulations of any country. Particularly relevant are laws relating to finance, customs, and excise duties, taxation, pensions, social security, employment and audit. Also important are statutes concerning evidence and limitation on action for claims. For example statutes bearing for accounting records may include Civil Evidence Acts, Value Added Tax Acts, Companies Acts, Consumer Protection Acts, Data Protection Acts, Financial Service Acts and the Limitation Acts. However, financial institutions in Malaysia were aware of the aforementioned Acts and regulations governing financial management, but records management has never been the priority. This is because there is no enforcement of practice. Sierra Leone like Malaysia does not enforce the laws and regulations governing records management practice even though many participants agreed that records management could give huge benefit and merits, many organisations do not take appropriate steps as the need is not pressing and no penalty levied for deliberate destruction of records. On this note, it is good that Public Records Act 1965 should be amended to suit the management of records in Sierra Leone, failing which the situation will be precarious.

c. Variable 3-Policies, Standards Procedures and Guidelines (PSPG)
Data collected were analysed by computing frequencies and percentages respectively of participants from identified response categories. The variable for this objective investigated the policies, standards and procedures and guidelines for the management of MoFED records. This variable serves as guidelines for the management of records for informed decision making at MoFED.

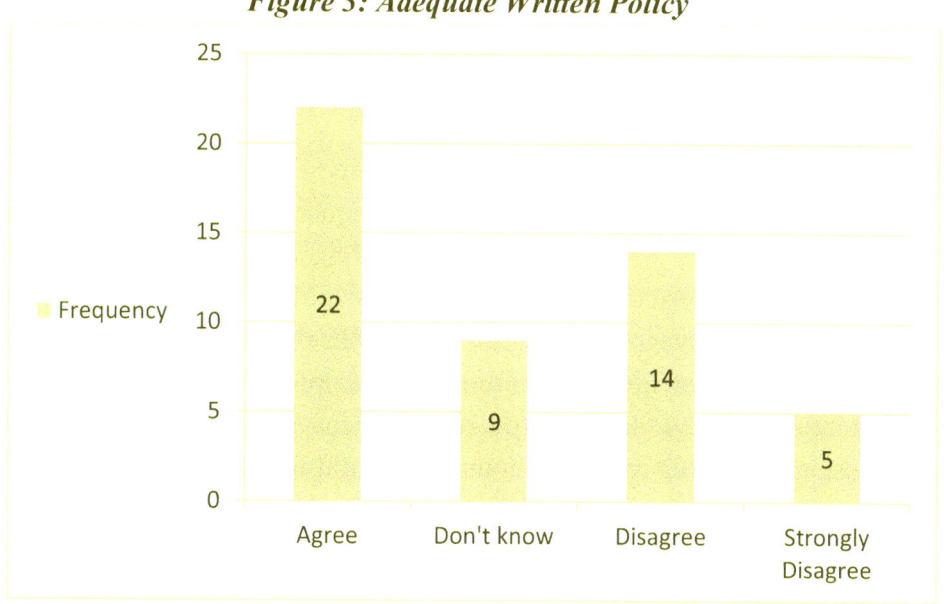

Figure 3: Adequate Written Policy

(Source: Field data on $9^{th}/04/2018$; SPSS version 16 and excel spreadsheet 2010)

Figure 3, illustrates that (44(f=22)) participants ''agreed'' that there is adequate provision of policies, standards and procedures for preparing and issuing retention schedules for the management of the ministries' financial/non-financial records and archive institution but not efficiently and effectively used. Eighteen percent of nine(18(f=9)) participants indicated 'don't know' which means that they are not aware of the provision of policies and procedures and do not know whether or not it is effectively and efficiently utilized for recordkeeping at the MoFED registry/administration. Twenty-eight percent of fourteen(28(f=14)) participants "disagreed," while (10(f=5)) participants "strongly disagreed" that the records management policies are adequately available and no participants "strongly agreed." However, the highest bar from the figure did reveal that there are adequate policies for the management of MoFED records but not effectively and efficiently utilised in enhancing their ultimate goal. Some participants agreed that since the Ministry is merged there are some of these policies, procedures and guidelines enshrined in the Government Budgeting and Accountability (GBA) Act 2005 for the management of the MoFED's financial records specifically and it is admissible in the Court of Law to prove evidence of transparency and accountability.

Discussion

The above figure shows that even though Sierra Leone is a developing country, the MoFED institution has adequate written policies or guidelines for the management of both financial and non-financial records but not effectively and efficiently utilized. The figure also portrays the presence of procedures/instructions that provide guidance on the management of financial records for example Financial Instruction, Accounting manual and records management guide but not utilized because the MoFED registry/administration did not hold or generate the Ministry's financial records. Figure 4 portrays that since the inception of records management in organisations, the ISO 15489(2001) standard was formulated in order to augment the records management operations which involved the following:
   a) the act of setting policies and standard;
   b) assigning responsibility and authorities;
   c) the establishment and promulgation of procedures and guidelines;

d) making provision for a range of services relating to the management and use of records;
e) designing, implementing, and administering specialized systems for managing records, and
f) integrating records management into business system and procedures

The policies set out the procedures and practices needed to control and manage records efficiently and effectively. In this light, developing and implementing a financial records management policy requires clarity about its aims and objectives irrespective of whether the system is manual or electronic. However, these figures above debunk that in most developing countries records keeping is not an organisation's key priority because it does not lead directly to profit making. The existence of policies serve as guidelines to facilitate actions and decisions to be taken. It is noted that advances in Information and Communication Technology(ICT) provide the opportunity for government to provide the delivery of information and services to citizens, and clientele in order to enhance good governance. And it is true that many organisations had policies before the institution of the reform programme but are often informal and oral in order to manage the institution's records effectively and efficiently. On this note, records policies are high-level statements that offer overall direction that is critical to the effectiveness of any records management project. However, these findings above debunk research findings that management of Public Services in Kenya(PSK) lacks policies, standards procedures and guidelines to underpin the effective and efficient management of financial records, in which case MoFED is an exception to this as it has adequate written policies but not effective and efficient in their implementation. As often noted, policies, rules, and procedures provide an environment conducive to proper records management. This is virtually what is carried out at the MoFED. It is interesting to note that during personal interview conducted in some departments within the MoFED, for instance the Accountant General Department(AGD) and Human Resource Management Office(HRMO) there is a similarity in the information supplied by staff on whether there are actual policies for managing records or not. The information received there was not quite different from the MoFED registry/administration unit, as there were policies on access and use of records, especially payroll records. In this case MoFED as a whole makes some effective utilization of both financial and non-financial records policies in order to achieve its responsibility/mandate enshrined in the "Government Budgeting and Accountability (GBA) Acts, 2005" and National Archives Act, 1965. Thus, these policies: retention policy for managing hard and soft copies; access authorisation are seldom used on a day-to-day basis.

Objective b-Facilities, Equipment and Supplies in relation to Disposition and Retention Schedule, and Monitoring and Compliances for Keeping Records at MoFED administration

d. Variable 4-Facilities, Equipment and Supplies (FES)

The variable for this objective investigated the provision of facilities, equipment and supplies. Participants were asked to indicate with a tick (√) those facilities, equipment, supplies and maintenance that are provided by MoFED administration/registry for the proper management of records. This variable depicts the storage materials for the preservation of MoFED records for both administrative and archival purposes. It can also mean the tool used to creating these records.

Figure 4: Facilities, Equipment and Supplies

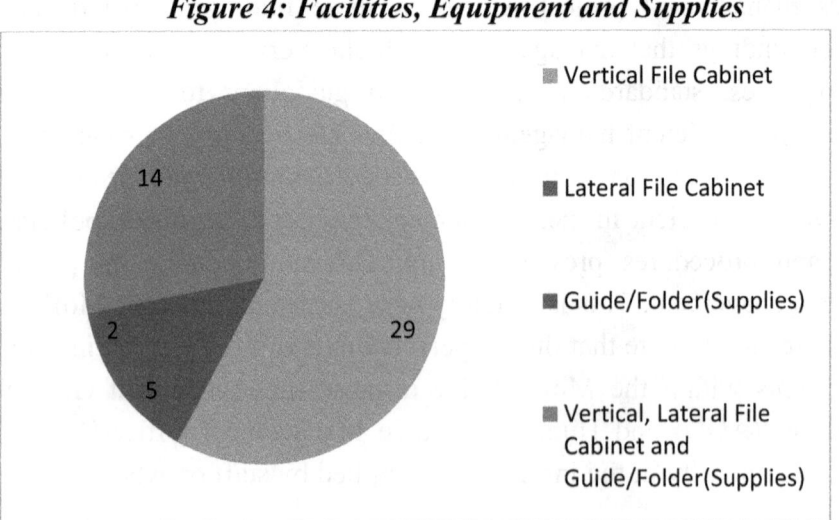

(Source: Field data on 9th/04/2018; SPSS version 16 and excel spreadsheet 2010)

The chart above shows that the largest orange portion of the chart indicated with (58(f=29)) participants that ''vertical file cabinet'' is in the MoFED registry/administration for preserving/managing records. While (28(f=14)) participants indicated that they have Vertical and Lateral file cabinets and Guides/Folders (Supplies) representing the green portion for managing/preserving records of MoFED administration. Ten percent of five(10(f=5)) participants in the red portion indicated that they have Lateral file cabinets only for preserving records. And (4(f=2)) blue portion of the chart represents Guides/Folders (Supplies) as the least indicator by participants.

Discussion

The findings noted that there is specific budget allocated but not very sufficient to maintain storage equipment provided at MoFED registry/administration for proper management of records. Figure 4 shows that MoFED registry/ administration does not have all the facilities, equipment and supplies stated in the questionnaire. Research findings has listed furniture, office equipment and supplies, that can be used for improving the records management operations which includes: library carts; telephone; public announcement system; desk lamps; desk; chairs; fax machines; book shelves; computers and printers; copy machines; file cabinets; scanners; desks; tables; shredders; cleaning materials; supply cabinets, face dust mask; diskette storage boxes; fax machine paper; work gloves; box labels; file folders and labels; computer diskettes; box tapes, three hole punch machines; staple, gums and removers; file charge-out cards; lab coat; and other general office supplies. Thus a lot of variables affect the way offices make their equipment selection: factors ranging from cost and required floor space to office appearance. Each office has unique and specific needs. The capabilities, merit, and demerits of different types of equipment must be measured in the context of those unique and specific system requirements.

Participants were further asked to state the types of facilities, supplies and equipment they need for the proper management of records, but not available. Many participants agreed that they need more facilities, supplies and equipment for proper management of records such as public announcement system, fax machine papers, shredders, computer diskettes, shelves, index cards are not provided and that, all the ones in their possession are not sufficiently provided. It was discovered that the MoFED administration has less equipment and these records storage equipment seems suitable as ascertained from participants' view. It was also discovered that the storage facilities for electronic financial records (e.g fire proof, safe and temperature control) are not very suitable according to the average response rate of participants. A good number of participants also said that they do not know whether or not these financial/vital records are protected against disaster and that there is no comprehensive and tested written disaster plan to protect the MoFED strategic financial system. On this note, an organisation should have a vital records protection programme as it will protect against some disasters and lessen the damage of these facilities, equipment and supplies, but disasters will still happen and the results can be devastating to an organisation unless it has implemented policies and procedures to protect its facilities, equipment and supplies. Thus, when disaster does occur there must be a disaster recovery programme designed to:

    a) minimize disruption of normal financial operation;
    b) prevent further escalation of this disruption;
    c) minimize the economic impact of the disaster;
    d) establish alternative operating procedures;
    e) train personnel in emergency procedures;
    f) recover/salvage organisational assets;
    g) and provide for rapid and smooth restoration of service.

On the other hand, subscribing to the views of other researchers that good financial records management could only be possible if there is a disaster recovery plan.

e. Variable 5-Monitoring and Compliance (MC)

The variable for this objective received information on monitoring and compliance with the phases of records keeping. This variable connotes the act of inspecting these records according to the life cycle management. It can be done by records managers, accountants, auditors, and archivists.

Figure 5: Monitoring and Compliance

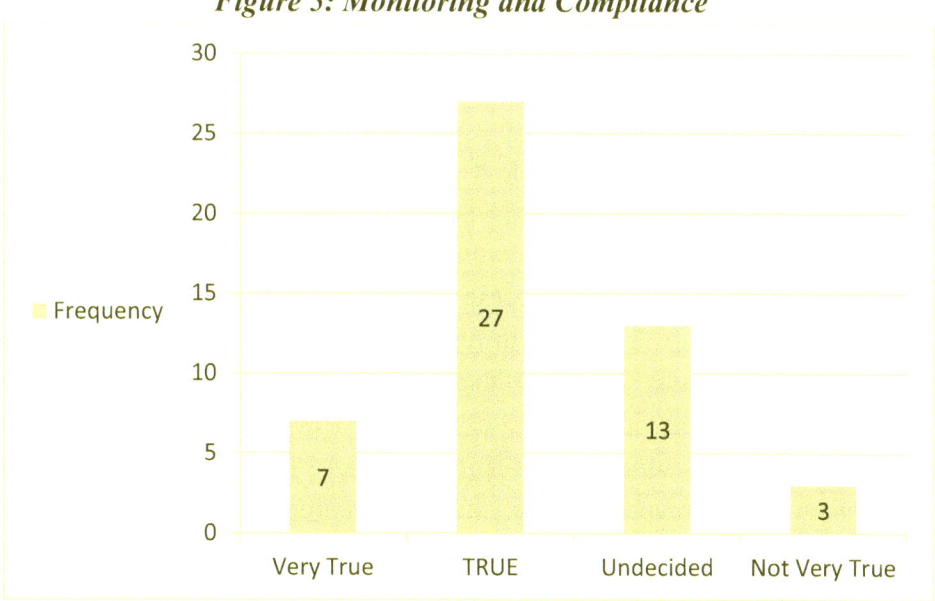

(Source: Field data on $9^{th}/04/2018$; SPSS version 16 and excel spreadsheet 2010)

Participants were asked to indicate their degree of agreement with regards officials' interest in the management of records. Fourteen percent of seven(14(f=7)) participants indicated "very true" that their officials do have interest in records management. Fifty-four percent of twenty-seven(54(f=27)) participants indicated "true" and (26(f=13)) participants indicated "undecided" while (6(f=3)) participants indicated "not very true" and no participants indicated "not true" as indicated in the questionnaire. In this case, the highest bar from the chart revealed that it is true that MoFED's senior officials did monitor the management of records with respect to the compliance of the phases of records keeping. At the Ministry, especially the MoFED registry/administration units, majority agreed that their officials have keen interest in records management. This was evidenced in the initial observation the researcher made on visits, as most of their records are organised and labelled both alphabetically and numerically which made the researcher consent that senior officials not only have interest but as well monitor the management of records. Thus each unit within MoFED institution has a records centre headed by senior records officer with records clerks which MoFED administration unit is no exception to this distinction of records management.

Discussion

Participants were further asked, if records are managed in accordance with the three phases of records keeping (active, semi-active, and in-active records). Majority of the twenty-seven(27) participants that agreed that their officials do take interest in records management also confirmed that they do manage records with respect to the three phases of records keeping. Participants indicated that active records are those that are generated and frequently used to carry out the organisation's day-to-day activities, whereas semi-active records are those not frequently used and are taken to the records centre; inactive records are those that are no longer used in official operations and are disposed of to the National Archives, but can be used for research purposes. The Ministry as a whole does similar things in the management of records in accordance with the three phases of record keeping (active, semi-active and in-active). And these records are monitored by Senior Records Managers, Archivists, Auditor General, Accountant General and Financial Secretary to ensure compliance with the three phases of records keeping. In that case, records management emanated from a specialised business discipline concerned with the systematic analysis and control of recorded information which include all information created, received, maintained or used by an organisation in accordance with its mission, and activities. In addendum, it is revealed that records management programme aims to manage the life cycle of records effectively to ensure that:

a) records are recognized and available to all organisation's staff who need to utilize them in support of its operations;

b) records transform to another stage as soon as they are no longer needed for active business;
c) records are only preserved as long as they have value for the owner or if they have ongoing historical value;
d) records of continuing value are protected against theft, fire, flood and other disasters;
e) records are stored in secured but economical accommodation;
f) each stage of the life cycle is managed in relation to their stages.

This practice at the MoFED confirms that the programme for managing financial records should be monitored on a regular basis. This should include systematic inspection of records managed by financial services in line ministries to ensure compliance with records management procedures and policies, identifying areas of strengths and weaknesses and measuring performance. This is in line with the opinion that the reports of the Auditor General also affect the management of financial records in institutions, and records management audit/inspection should be carried out on financial records at regular intervals, two or three times a year. Also, other scholar contented that monitoring systems in Sierra Leone concerning the management of records are inadequate and information is difficult to access; proper audit system is virtually ineffective and very costly for public institutions. Thus, Moore admonished that monitoring records should be robust for proper records management procedures in Ministries, Departments, and Agencies (MDAs) and MoFED institution is no exception.

f. Variable 6-Disposition and Retention Schedule (DRS)
The variable for this objective investigated disposition and retention procedures. Participants were asked to indicate the relevance of the statement as to whether or not MoFED registry/administration unit has a disposition and retention schedule in the management of records. This variable shows the way records are disposed of and retained at MoFED administration according to records management policies.

Figure 6: Disposition and Retention Schedule

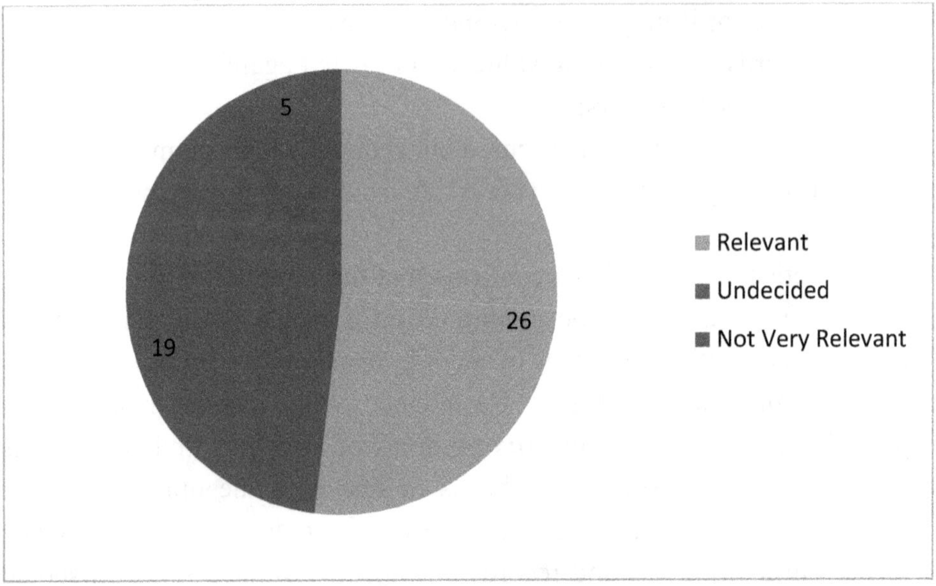

[Pie chart showing: Relevant = 26, Undecided = 19, Not Very Relevant = 5]

(Source: Field data on 9th/o4/2018; SPSS version 16 and excel spreadsheet 2010)

From figure 6, (52(f-26)) participants indicated "relevant" which represents the largest portion of the orange sector; (38(f=19)) participants indicated "undecided" which means that they are not quite *au fait* with the management of records at MoFED or do not practice records management according to the prescribed records management retention and disposition schedule of MoFED institution; and (10(f=5)) participants indicated "not very relevant" that they dispose of records and retain some; and no participant indicated "very relevant" and "not relevant" respectively. However, MoFED does retain records and dispose of some to the National Archives that could be useful in the future for national development (ie the MoFED administration division does play active role in the disposition and retention procedure).

Discussion

In an open-ended question, participants were further asked about the period of time records are retained before disposition. Retention period varies virtually from one department/unit to another within the Ministry. Some of the stated periods are: 1-6 years for financial records; 3 years, 5 years, 7 years, 10 years, and 25 years for non-financial records. Some participants revealed that they do retain records for long while others have no specified time. From these ratings, it is the researcher's observation that those who said "no specific time" do not really understand the practice of retention and disposition of records in the MoFED registry/administration. From the interview conducted with some personnel in this division, there is evidence of retention as well as disposition practice of records, as though the duration of time was a bone of contention. However, twenty-six(26) of the participants in the MoFED registry/administration division stated the duration period as seven(7) years of retention. The researcher in turn consented to participants' view at the MoFED institution, with the observation that retention and disposition of records is a continuous practice within the Ministry.

It is contended that non-financial and financial records are managed in the same way; the only difference is some financial records have shorter lives than other records. It further stated both financial and non-financial records can be appraised, have a retention period ranging from 1-25 years and can be archived for future use. However, the retention period for most financial records is 1, 2 and 6 years respectively. Participants were further asked to state the disposition procedures used by them. The aspect of disposition identified at MoFED registry/administration was that semi-current records are transferred to the records centre and the non-current records that do have historical value are bound and sent to the National Archives since the amalgamation of the Ministry in 2007. However, most records and data are captured for the day-to-day running of the Ministry.

About the retention procedures, many participants opined that records are kept in folders marked and placed in a special cabinet or stored in hard and soft copies. Some of these records include all ministerial, departmental and agency's files requesting for grant approval. For instance correspondences of the Office of the President files, Ministry of

Education, Science and Technology, Ministry of Agriculture and Food Security, and public debt bulletins are all stacked on shelves or in cabinets because information contained therein are of enduring value. Other records such as civil service personnel are stacked in glass cabinets until the retirement age of sixty(60) years before they are qualified for archives. The administration unit also draws schedules in consultation with senior staff of respective units, especially the Human Resource Management Office(HRMO). All reports are kept. Personnel files are removed from current storage and after payment of pensionable benefits, they would be kept in a store room/records centre. The MoFED registry/administration division often takes decision to retain personnel files until they are transferred to the National Records Centre. In support of the view of records life cycle management, it is affirmed that the process of managing records is frequently associated with living organisms as they can be reproduced, live and are being used, become obsolescence and can be retired, died and taken to Archive institutions for preservation. In this case, a robust disposal policy is critical for good records management and good business. One should always consider the act of destroying worthless information. Also, many scholars claimed that any organisation should manage financial records throughout their life, from the point of creation to their ultimate disposition.

Further, it is noted that the objective of records management is to ensure their proper creation, use, storage, receipt, short and long term retention and disposal, their protection and maintenance, during and after their operational utilization. For documents of historical or research value, it is not economical to destroy non-current records as soon as they attain their retention period. This could provide space for records management equipment kept for current and semi-current records. Thus the methods and procedures mandating for the destruction of records vary from information medium and extent of confidentiality of records.

Participants were also asked to indicate the manner in which their records are preserved, whether manual or electronic. Thirty-one (31) participants indicated that they preserved more of manual records than electronic records. Manual format records are received, sorted out, labeled and stacked on shelves in a cabinet. Others revealed that records are kept in a cool (air conditioning), secure and dry place. For manual records, hard copies are filed in big lever-arch files and kept in both metal and glass cabinets. And electronic records are kept on network savers in the ICT and some other units. Similarly, images of pdf are kept on back-up drives and on savers. Electronic mail correspondences are kept on storage by Internet service providers in the ICT department only.

A survey report on Ho Polytechnic, a tertiary institution in Ghana, observed that the institution's records management is shifting form manual to electronic system by using computers and Internet facilities. Thus, this allows users to complete and summit the information on time. The electronic filing system prevents users from making serious mistakes that could affect the operations and image of the institution. The decision should be based on probability of access to resources versus the total cost of maintenance. Thus the general option for storage includes online and offline. Records accessed most should be stored online while records accessed least are stored offline. After determining the place records are to be stored, one should determine the manner they (records) can be accessed. This only depends on the types of records and the media format chosen.

Thus, appropriate media and system should be selected for maintaining records over a period of time. In this scenario files should frequently be migrated to new media when the need arises within a stated period of time. In subscription to the above, the researcher discovered that MoFED has both manual and electronic records retention and disposition practice in the management of its records. This is evident in the retrieval of most of the records from MoFED's website to augment the research in question.

Objective c- Users, Training and Qualifications/Competencies in overcoming the challenges at MoFED registry/administration

This objective investigated the users of records, security and training competencies. Participants were asked to state the users of their records. The users as mentioned by participants vary from one unit/division to another. The users of MoFED records are highlighted thus: Ministers; Deputy Ministers; the President, Financial Secretary; Development Secretary; Contract Officers/Local Technical Assistant(LTAs); Administrative Staff, Civil Servants; Accountant General; Donor Agents/Officers; Statisticians; Internal and External Auditors; Records Practitioners; Researchers; House of Parliament; Anti- Corruption Commission(ACC); MDAs; and the public.

The researcher observed that not only the usual users of public records in Sierra Leone are given the priority to access and utilise records but donors providing funds can also access and utilise records of the Ministry. This is evident in the Right to Access Information (RAI) Act, 2013 which allows the general public to request for government records or information for the conduct of business activities. The main purpose of the Act is to provide for the disclosure of information held by public authorities or by persons providing services for them and for other related matters.

Discussion

Based on the aforementioned users of records, the researcher subscribed that records are systematic management of administrative records significance in order to protect and preserve them as evidence of actions; to support future activities and business decisions and ensure accountability; to present and future stakeholders and customers. In this regard, it is observed that records management programme intends to manage the life cycle of records effectively to ensure that records are known and available to all the agency's staff who need to use them as supportive operation. Thus, MoFED records users utilize these records to further the operations of the Ministry to achieving its ultimate goal.

g. Variable 7-Challenges for Managing Records (CMR)

Further, participants were asked about the challenges facing MoFED registry/administration staff in managing records. This variable indicates the problems faced by MoFED administration staff in managing records.

Figure 7: Challenges in Managing Records

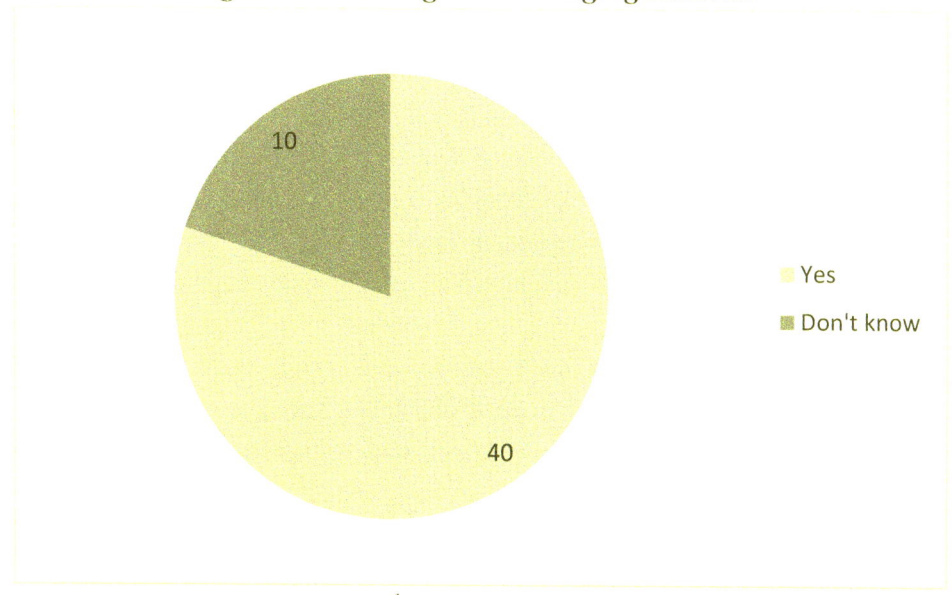

(Source: Field data on $9^{th}/04/2018$; SPSS version 16 and excel spreadsheet 2010)

From figure 7 (80(f=40)) participants indicated "yes" that they are faced with some challenges and (20(f=10)) participants in the red sector indicated that they do not know whether there are challenges or not and no participants indicated "no" challenges. Diving into this issue proper, it is revealed that staff face some challenges in the management of records which include inadequate trained and qualified records personnel at middle level, inadequate materials like file covers, insufficient funds, inadequate space, insufficient logistical support, and slow Internet service. This situation warranted the researcher to interrogate record officers. Staff responded that the Ministry is not fully capacitated for the proper management of records. However modalities are in place to revamp this situation, but the major challenge being inadequate funding, space and trained and qualified records staff.

Discussion

There are some challenges facing records management users in managing records in developing countries which include, lack of resources, space constraints, high staff turnover, specific approaches to records and archives management. It is further stated that two prominent issues need to be addressed for records management to develop given the prestige that the profession deserves. These are lack of accessible training programmes and the need for holistic and targeted awareness programmes at all administrative levels of any organisation, and the public in general. On this note, research has found that management population services in Kenya faced a plethora of challenges, the major being, lack of policies, standard procedures and guidelines to enhance the effective and efficient management of financial records. There are other issues such as low priority accorded to records management, absence of records management culture, inadequate skills for managing both manual and electronic record formats. These are similar to the management of records by MoFED registry/administration and MoFED in general.

h. Variable 8-Missing, Lost, or Damaged Records (MLDR)

Furthermore, participants were asked whether there are cases of missing, lost, or damaged records or files and users are educated on the use of records. This variable depicts the way records are lost, missing/damaged at MoFED administration in the wake of management.

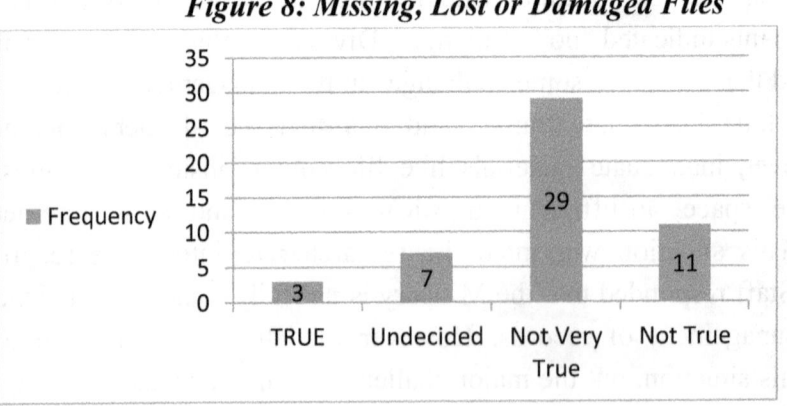

Figure 8: Missing, Lost or Damaged Files

(Source: Field data on 9th/04/2018; SPSS version 16 and excel spreadsheet 2010)

From figure 8, it is "true" that (6(f=3)) participants indicated that there are cases of missing, misplaced, lost or damaged records; and (14(f=7)) participants indicated "undecided" that there are missing, misplaced, lost or damaged nor missing or lost records at MoFED administration. Fifty-eight percent of twenty-nine(58(f=29)) participants indicated "not very true" while (22(f=11)) indicated "not true" for missing, misplaced, lost or damaged records or files at MoFED registry/administration and no participants indicated "very true" for missing, misplace, lost or damaged records or files. Thus the longest bar from the chart reveals that there are not always missing, misplaced, lost or damaged records at MoFED administration because records are highly regarded as valued commodity in this institution.

Discussion

The symptoms of poor records management are as follows: inaccurate information; duplication of records, not knowing the least version; complex filing system difficult to use; waste of time looking for records and information when they are not properly organised; records are always prone to loss or damage; Ubiquitous records; the waste of space due to unwanted storing records; in-conducive working environment; poor decision making; the legislative requirement is not adhered to; security is often lacking; and user dissatisfaction.

On the contrary, it is contended that there were cases of missing, misplaced, loss of damaged records at Sierra Leone public sector organisations and MoFED registry/administration is not an exception based on figure 9. Against this background, some government officials have been accused of embezzling funds simply because the documents portraying the expenditure could not be located. Thus, well-managed records are essential to overcome economic crimes and protect the innocent. Financial records management programmes should enable the physical and logical control of records and prevent unauthorised access, tampering, loss or destruction, be it intentional or accidental.

i. Variable 9-Qualifications/ Competencies (Q/C)

Furthermore, participants were asked to indicate their degree of justification to the statement that MoFED registry/administration staff have qualifications/competencies in managing both financial and non-financial records. This variable shows the degree of experience via formal training in the management of records at MoFED.

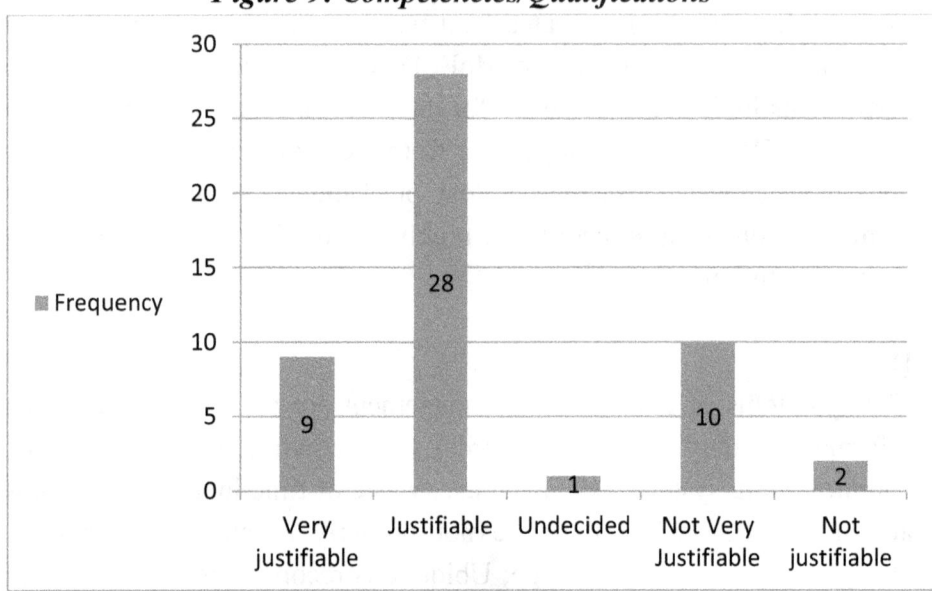

Figure 9: Competencies/Qualifications

(Source: Field data on $9^{th}/04/2018$; SPSS version 16 and excel spreadsheet 2010)

From figure 9 (18(f=9)) participants indicated "very justifiable", (56(f=28)) participants indicated "justifiable", (2(f=1)) participants indicated "undecided", (20(f=10)) participants indicated "not very justifiable" and (4(f=2)) participants indicated "not justifiable" that MoFED registry/administration staff have qualifications/competencies in the management of records. On the average, the highest bar represents the highest percentage of participants that indicated MoFED registry/administration staff have qualifications/competencies in managing records.

Discussion

From figure 9, the highest bar reveals that it is very justifiable that MoFED staff have qualifications/competencies in managing records. Most of the staff have higher educational standards with basic records management training at least to manage the MoFED registry/administration records. Staff, including records officers and their clerks are all competent with basic computer skills in the management of MoFED records. However, competence could make possible to identify the required educational standard, training needs, level of experience and, whenever possible, practical expertise required by staff responsible for managing financial records. Where there is a relevant scheme of service in place of records staff, job specification must incorporate the qualifications specified by the scheme. It is also noted that the role of records and accounts staff is dealt with only in relation to their responsibilities for managing financial records. The competencies of each grade level, in terms of its responsibilities, entry qualifications, career development and training requirements should be defined carefully and clearly. Thus, for both records and accounting staff an important concept is that staff exercising the same level of responsibilities should form part of the same grade. On the same token, in many countries such as the Republic of South Africa, the function of managing current, semi-current and non-current records is separated and falls to both accounting and records staff. This can be further divided into national records and archives institutions, and the Ministry of Finance, Treasury, and the line Ministry staff in both the records and accounting cadre. Thus, it is critical for the effective management of financial system that those staff with the responsibility of managing records has a clear career path with those staff with appropriate grade levels and remuneration.

j. Variable 10-Training Facilities (TF)

Participants were questioned as to the type of training facilities imparted to users especially MoFED administration staff. This variable portrays the act of undergoing on the job training on the records management system at MoFED administration.

Figure 10: Training Facilities

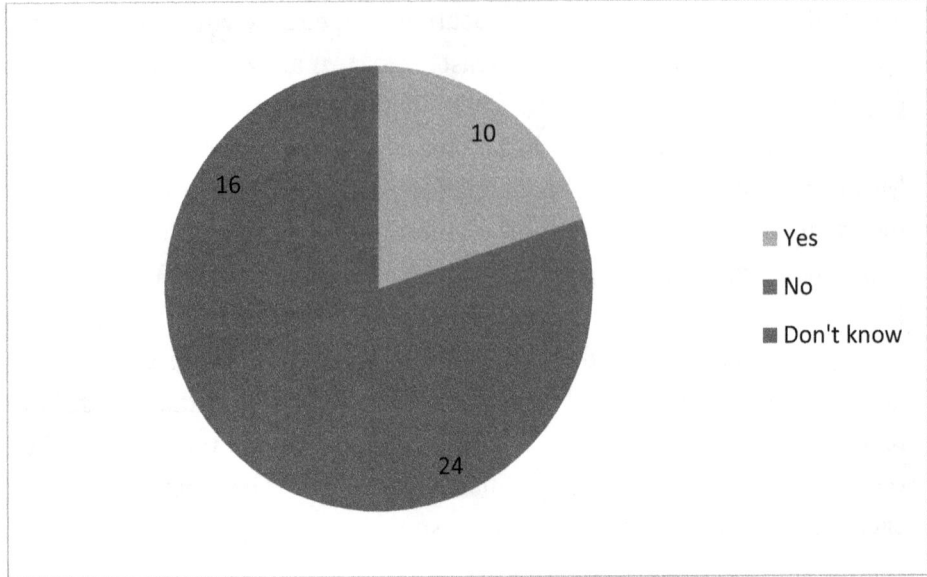

(Source: Field data on $9^{th}/04/2018$; SPSS version 16 and excel spreadsheet 2010)

From figure10 (20(f=10)) participants which represented the orange portion stated that "yes" training is conducted for users while (48(f=24)) participants indicated that no training is conducted for the management of records and (32(f=16)) participants indicated "don't know" whether training is provided or not for users.

Discussion

From figure 10, it is evident that some participants agreed that there are training facilities for users/staff at MoFED registry/administration for the management of records. On this note, induction training should be provided in a timely fashion to all civil servants for the management of records. The basic guidance on the rule and regulations governing the creation and handling of records, particularly the legal responsibilities conferred on all staff by the National Records and Archives Act should be included. In addition, records staff should receive more detailed guidance in their induction training to help them understand the structure and duties of the government records management system. Against this background, However, there are still problems of training facilities for records staff in particular on both paper and electronic records in Sierra Leone. In support of this, scholars recommended in their study on Ho Polytechnic, a tertiary institution in Ghana that despite sound records practice they still have some gaps in the area of training, supervision and control on records management skills for all relevant employees in order to improve better records management performance which MoFED is no exception. The Record Archivist of South Africa is mandated to give proper training on management of records to records practitioners or information practitioners at the public sector as this would improve the performance of Ministries, Departments and Agencies in enhancing governance.

The researcher is of the view that without such training at the MoFED, it will not achieve its aims and objectives. However, few participants did state that there is some aspect of basic records management training but only for clerical staff gaining entrance into the Ministry during the induction training exercise. Records management workshop is done seldomly . Thus, from the analysis above, MoFED does undertake some aspects of training programmes on the life cycle of records; and guidance for records management performance for the proper management of financial and non-financial records. However, in the closed interview conducted with some staff at the Accountant General Department (AGD), (Messrs Francis Turay and Joseph Sesay, and Mrs. Fatmata Kamara), there are some aspects of life cycle records management training for all categories of staff. The reason being, they manage records that are sensitive in nature and thus should not be held by any other unit in order to prevent duplicity in records management functions. This is inconsistent with the researcher's view as the MoFED registry/ administration is the epicentre of all administrative affairs and thus should also hold records of financial value in order to achieve transparency.

Objective d-Information and Communication Technology (ICTs) and Electronic Records Management Policy at MoFED administration

k. Variable 11-Information Communication Technologies (ICTs)

The variable depicting this objective investigated issues relating to Information and Communication Technologies (ICTs). This is the use of computers, memory sticks, and diskette to create and store records of enduring value.

Figure 11: ICTs Provision

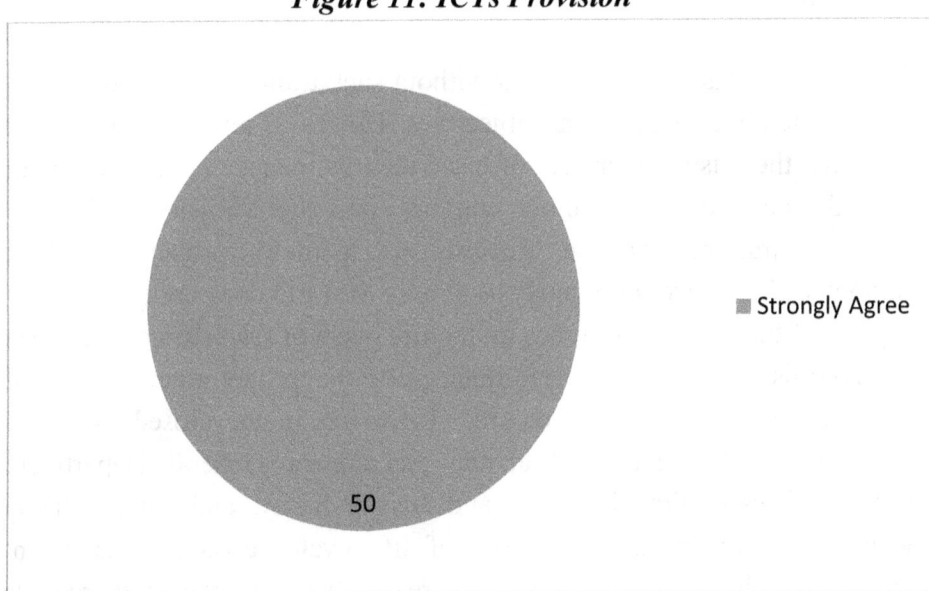

(Source: Field data on $9^{th}/04/2018$; SPSS version 16 and excel spreadsheet 2010)

Figure 11 shows that 100(f=50) participants indicated the existence of ICTs in the MoFED institution. Thus, all participants were of the notion that MoFED does have ICTs. Participants at MoFED registry/administration division did agree that ICTs are at the Ministry and are being used for managing records.

Discussion

The aforementioned analysis portrays that all the participants strongly agreed that there is an ICTs unit at MoFED providing related services to all departments within the Ministry of Finance and Economic Development. It is asserted that there are some guidelines for the management of electronic records from the National Archives of South Africa, and a lot of the government bodies have implemented electronic management systems, but majority of electronic records are yet to be managed in terms of records management principles in these institutions. On this same premise, It is also stated that the emergent implementation of new technology and their growing adoption and use in records and archival institutions is gradually changing the way organisations work, make decision, communicate, and even document their activities. Gregory admonished records practitioners to pay attention to electronic formats. Many theorist has listed such electronic records as e-mail, voicemail, Geographic Information System (GIS), web-pages, work process document, spreadsheet, database, digital image, video and audio files. It is ardently contended that anyone dealing with electronic records should obtain relevant guidelines issued by records professional bodies.

However, despite the possibility of artificial/human interference in the distortion of electronically recorded information, there is also unplanned natural disaster interference. Thus, there need to be a disaster recovery programme to be initiated by records managers in collaboration with other personnel in the organisation. This is the opposite at MoFED as indicated by participants that there is no disaster recovery programme for computerised financial system. On this note electronic records management is the greatest professional challenge to archivists and records managers in developing countries, especially in sub-Sahara Africa since the 1990s. It has been observed that electronic records possess certain challenges and implications particularly the appraisal of electronic records to archivists. Thus, with the development of computers, records are generated in electronic format. However, the advent of electronic records keeping will raise issues technically which focus on the selection of hardware and software, maintenance system, upgrading and training system. On the other hand, the managerial issues will deal with information technology policy, training of staff and resource sharing. These key enablers of electronic records need to be considered in order to establish effective electronic management programmes. In this case, electronic records are easily manipulated and overwritten. Once the database is created and networked, such security measures should be needed to prevent unauthorized access to such records particularly, financial records. This is evident in the provision of special ICT units that oversee the operations of computer devices and ensure the proper maintenance of both hardware and software systems at MoFED. It also provides training facilities to staff. The system performance is regularly checked and virus protection often provided. It has further asserted that there are two main areas of data protection requirements apart from the general one: the ability of electronic records to satisfy legal requirements and the admissibility of electronic records as evidence. Thus, some participants agreed that MoFED records, especially financial records, are admissible/allowed in the court of law as evidence to testify against guilt.

l. Variable 12-Electronic Records Management Policies (ERMP)

Variable 12 shows participants' affirmation about the laid down policy for the management of electronic records. This entails disposition and retention policies, monitoring and compliance, the use of password for Internet access to control the electronic use in managing records etc.

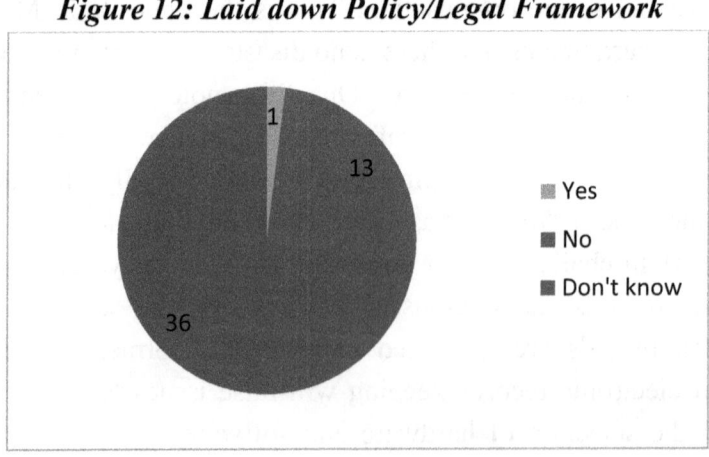

Figure 12: Laid down Policy/Legal Framework

(Source: Field data on 9th/04/2018; SPSS version 16 and excel spreadsheet 2010)

From figure 12, (72(f=36)) participants indicated "don't know" that there is either a laid down policy or not for the management of electronic record. Also (26(f=13)) participants stated "no" that there is no laid down policy for management of records. While (2(f=1)) participant stated "yes" that there is a laid down policy for the management of electronic records at MoFED registry/administration.

Discussion

I has been advanced that policies and guidelines should be developed to provide for the retention and disposition of all electronic records, which include those recorded on both mainframe and mini-frame computers. They further stated that the National Archives in the UK published two sets of functional guidelines to promote the development of electronic records management software market (1999-2002). They have also run a programme to evaluate products against the 2002 requirements. These requirements were initially formulated in collaboration with the central government as they have been taken up with enthusiasm by many parts of the wider public sector in the UK and in other parts of the world. However, the most up-to-date guideline is the "MoReq2", published in February, 2008. On this same premises, the existence of policies serve as guidelines to facilitate actions and decisions to be taken. It is noted that advances in Information and Communication Technology (ICT) provide the opportunity for government to improve its delivery of information and services to citizens and business to streamline public sector functions, and increase public participation in governance. Their findings revealed that not all governments possess an electronic records management policy that is clear, complete, and easy to implement. Thus, organisations are using policies provided by Malaysian Administrative Modernisation and Management planning Unit (MAMPU) and the National Archives of Malaysia(NAM) with some modifications to suit their needs. On the other hand, the number of organisations that carry out electronic records without any policy in place is alarming. In this vein, electronic records management carried out in some organisations is merely based on their instinct and initiative; far from complying with the international standards of best practice in Malaysia of which MoFED, Sierra Leone is no exception. The "White Paper of KSHS" maintained that electronic records keeping under the responsibility of agencies should ensure that records keeping policies and procedures are developed and implemented as part of overall business plans. This is on the contrary at MoFED administration as many participants indicated that it is not to their knowledge that a laid down electronic records management policy exists.

On this same token, the state Archive and Records of New South Wales Policy on Electronic Records keeping asserted that business conducted in electronic environment should be documented properly to meet the requirements of operational and community accountability. This entails making and keeping records in an electronic system to advance the use of machine learning for the automation of records classification and disposal system. Indeed there are already commercial records management products available that use machine learning such as auto-classification to improve search. The policy document of State Archives and Records of New South Wales(NSW) has made tremendous improvement across NSW government, in transforming from desktop application and migrating their email, document storage, project management, collaboration and other business software to software as-a-service platform like the Microsoft Office 365. Some organisations have started using this product, but records practitioners in these organisations are amongst the least to find out. MoFED is yet to do so.

Objective e-Good Governance, Accountability, Transparency and proper records keeping at MoFED Administration and National Archive

m. Variable 13-Good Governance, Accountability and Transparency (GGAT)

The variable depicting figure 14 shows good governance, accountability, and transparency and proper records keeping. This variable entails the delivering of efficient financial public service to enhance sustainable development at MoFED institution. This can only be possible through sound records keeping.

Figure 13: Good Governance, Accountability and Transparency

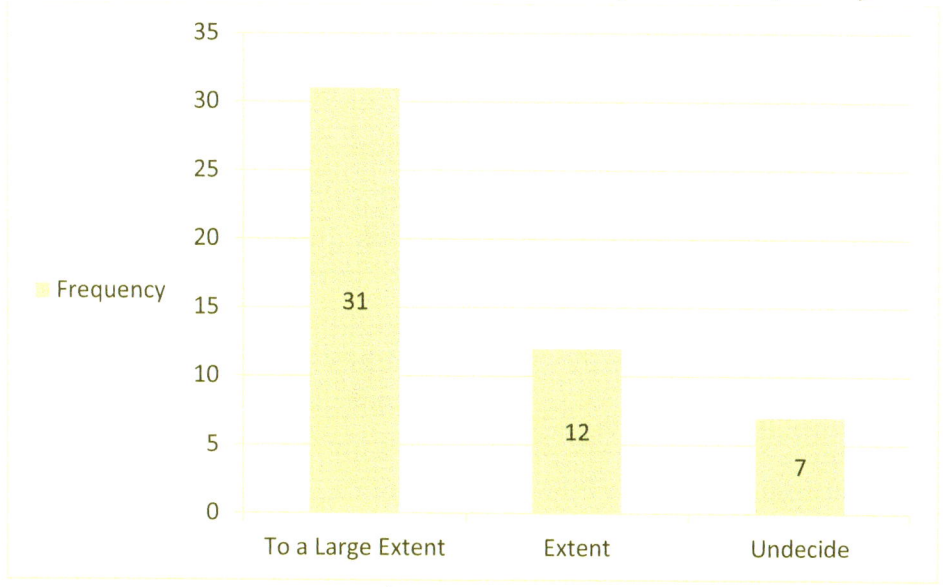

(Source: Field data on 9th/04/2018; SPSS version 16 and excel spreadsheet 2010)

Figure 13 statistic reveals that a majority (62(f=31)) participants are of the view that sound records keeping enhances good governance, accountability and transparency in varied ways. While (24(f=12)) participants responded that good records keeping system enables good governance, transparency and accountability and (14(f=7)) participants were "undecided" whether or not good records keeping enhances good governance, transparency and accountability and no participants indicated "not to a large extent" and "not extent" respectively. Thus, the highest bar from the chart reveals that good records keeping at MoFED organisation, administration unit to be specific enhances governance, accountability and transparency.

Discussion

Participants further indicated that the sound delivery of records services by MoFED registry/administration can: enhance the management of government funds; help generate Gross National Income(GNI)/Gross Domestic Product(GDP) and ensure equitable distribution of national resources; facilitate immediate and accurate decision making and taking; provide evidence for economic transactions; promote intellectual control systems; improve internal and external operating systems; help achieve research and development aspirations(for e.g the history and development of MoFED institution can be used for further development); enhance quick and sound decision making and expedience retrieval of information for developmental purposes; protect certain vital/financial information the institution has about its business transactions; ensure the protection of staff information for e.g. payroll, retirement benefit and other confidential matters; prevent bad governance and promote transparency; enhance policy makers in making informed decision; promote prudent financial management through tackling fraud and promoting climate of trust; discourage mismanagement of consolidated funds and ensure equitable distribution of these funds to varied Ministries, Departments and Agencies(MDAs) in any democratic states; strengthen the protection of human rights, the rule of law, and fair and equal treatment of citizens; and consistently help achieve efficiency, effectiveness and productivity in MoFED institution.

These findings are consistent with the views of some scholars who advanced that advocating for good governance should be part of records and archives management profession. As it is only when certain principles are applied to the process of financial records identification which could be easily retrieved for decision making in public sector financial institutions , will the concept of good governance and accountability be meaningful.

It is asserted that there is a positive correlation between governance and records keeping which support the hypothesis and as well agrees with the views of participants. For example in Ghana effective management of public sector financial information is a critical factor in providing capacity for public sector efficiency and good governance. This view supports an emerging trend in public sector management system which provides the evidence required to support transparency and accountability and at the same time inform the effective management of consolidated funds. They facilitate the achievement of accountability and transparency in public and private administrations. Thus, it is hard for government to achieve good governance without efficient records keeping systems in place.

It is also affirmed that records are virtually significant to every aspect of the governance process. It concedes to the expressed notion that records and the evidence they contain, are the instruments which government promotes the environment of trust and demonstrates an overall commitment to good governance. However, a government body that is unable to provide the right information at the right time through Right to Access Information (RAI) law and ideas improvement preceding its introduction adversely affects the citizens' rights to participate in the decision process. Also sound records management is of immense importance to this process. Accountability is defined as fundamental to good governance. It is a process that allows people to measure and verify the performance of government. Financial accountability is a critical component of accountable government. It involves legislative control of executive through budgets and accounts. It is further stated that weakness in financial accountability is generally linked to week cash management, auditing, and the management of financial records. From a study that aimed at evaluating the importance of financial records keeping in achieving good governance with emphasis on public sector organisations drawing experiences from Nigeria and some other African countries. The study found out that despite efforts to institute comprehensive programmes of financial and structural changes via varied economic policy reforms, some financial records are still buried and inaccessible and thus could be attributed to poor organisational structure and management of records. Further studies maintained that one of the pillars of good governance and democracy was transparency, probity and accountability, which can only be achieved via effective records management system. Furthermore, financial records are produced virtually in all areas of financial management. If these records are not well managed, financial functions suffer. In this light, financial records management and records management are closely related. And the breakdown of financial system is often related to breakdown in records management. Thus, records management reinforces financial control and support accountability and transparency. The ability to reveal who did what, why and how, is a powerful means of deterring individuals from engaging in corruption, thus enforcing accountability. However, However, in Sierra Leone, being the subject of study, cannot ensure accountability and transparency in a bad condition of operationalized system of the Right to Access Information(RAI) or the Open Government Initiatives(OGI) because of the following factors which need to be addressed: the 1965 National Public Archive Law; ensuring at least a records centre in each of the four regions of the country; embarking on clearing of massive backlog of closed files and other documents currently occupying expensive office space across the public service; working towards improved records management cadre; restructuring records office systems across the public service; producing retention schedules for various types of records(for e.g financial, human resources, health, legal; and training of records staff on the management of both paper and electronic system.

In support of the above factors, there is a culture of records keeping and top management support for both records keeping and public service at MoFED. If there is contrary, it will distort the effective functioning of government activities which could deter accountability, transparency, and good governance. At MoFED, it was revealed that the proper management of both financial and non-financial records is critical to support economic development and provide accountability, transparency, and good governance. These are basic fundamental variables that strengthen democracy, improve financial service delivery and reduce poverty as one of the functions of MoFED in Sierra Leone. Thus, without access to information there is no transparency; without transparency, accountability cannot be expected; and without accountability and transparency democratic credentials are incomplete.

n. Variable14- MoFED Administration and National Archives (MoFEDR/A&NA)

This variable depicts in figure15, reveals the relationship between MoFED registry/ administration and the National Archives. MoFED administration manages current records while National Archives manage non-current records for posterity.

Figure 14: MoFED registry/administration and National Archives

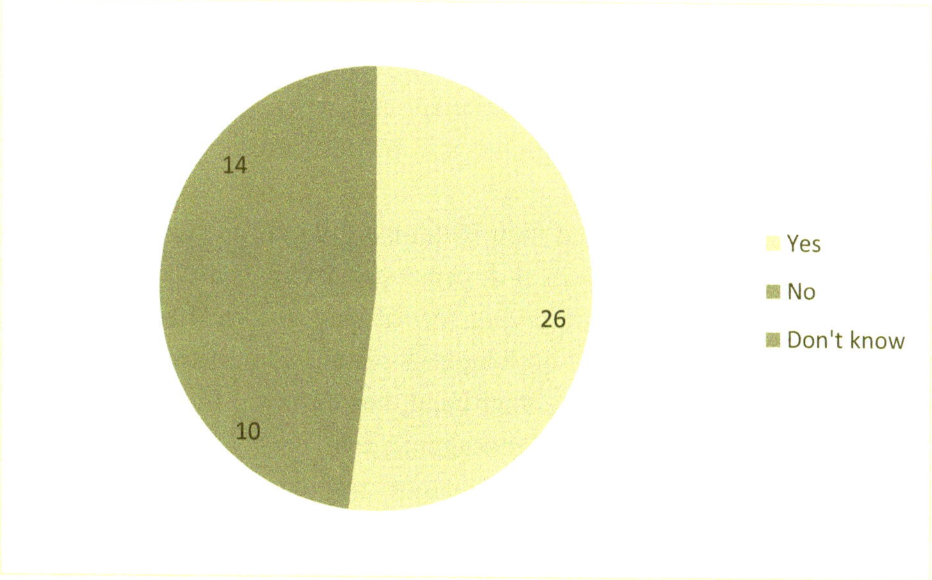

(Source: Field data on 9th/04/2018; SPSS version 16 and excel spreadsheet 2010)

From figure 14, (52(f=26)) participants as indicated in the orange portion of the sector revealed that there is a relationship between MoFED administration unit and the National Public Archives. These are the corporate memory of the Ministry, as posited by participants that have research value. On the other hand, (20(f=10)) participants in the red sector of the chart indicated "no" relationship between MoFED administration/registry and National Archives. Also (28(f=14)) participants as portrayed in the blue sector of the chart indicated "don't know" whether or not there is a relationship between MoFED registry/administration unit and the National Archives. Perhaps the second view either forgot to indicate or due to ignorance, did not comprehend the role of the National Archives in national development.

Discussion

In support of the above analysis, there are certain similarities and differences of the archives and records professions. For similarities both: are called to identify which documents(records) they will manage; need to be careful about maintaining the physical and intellectual integrity of records in their care; describe and arrange records to provide access as well as contextual information; observe necessary legislation regarding disposal, privacy, intellectual property, and other issues; and maintain the physical, including the digital condition of records.

It is further maintained that their differences could be based largely on cultural, societal, and historical dimensions. Archives are apolitical, and cannot be seen only as preserving records for historical research or as warehouses for old records no longer in current administrative use. And records management, on the other hand, has emerged from a modernist, late capitalist philosophy of management in both private and public entities embarking on efficiency, competitive advantage, and strategic value, increase of profit and avoidance of loss. On the other hand, archives and records have the same challenges. They include lack of resources, space constraints, high staff turnover, lack of accessible training and targeted awareness programmes at all administrative level of any organisation and specific approaches to records and archives management institutions. It is also posited that the key to administrative advancement is the effective caring for information. Archival records should be preserved in facilities and equipment designed to maintain their permanent life, to discourage further deterioration and assure that records maintain their utility condition. From the aforementioned Ngulube (2006) highlighted that: *each new country has to establish its own identity. It must select elements of its history, culture, and act as a symbol of national unity in public settings, on money, stamps, flags, government building, etc to show the people what they have in common as a united country and also what they can be proud of to possess together as a fellow countrymen(p.108).*

In this case a well organised archives office and good records management are paramount for the furtherance of administrative efficiency and enhancing socio-economic development. On the other hand the process of managing records is often associated with a living organism, as they can be reproduced, and are being used, become aged and can be retired, died and taken to National Archives institutions for preservation, which can be used for historical and research purposes. And it is only an Archival institution that does external monitoring across governments departments according to agreed inspection plans. This mandate extends to the act of drafting records retention policy that can be included in the national constitution in countries such as South Africa, Ghana, Kenya and Sierra Leone. Records managers and Archivists in the public sector should work in tandem to achieve national development. Thus, the researcher subscribes to the notion of the three authors that archival institutions are very pivotal for national development, Sierra Leone to be specific. However, it is noted that records management field emanated from the archival profession during the 1950's and the proceeding years achieved a distinct professional identity in its own rights. Nevertheless, the two professions are common in identity, and records managers need a good understanding of archival principles and practices in order to develop a comprehensive records management programme. In the perspective of governments in sub-Sahara African countries, the two professions are not far-fetched. Nengomasha further stated that they manage the same records media; both are concerned with the quality of records and they use the same system and techniques to augment their accessions. Thus, the above figures revealed that there is official relationship as the National Archives are a statutory body responsible for the handling of government records across the board which MoFED is no exception.

3. Z-SCORE AND PROBABILITY VALUE TEST FOR THE VARIABLES

The aforementioned variables are statistically tested via the use of certain parameters such as Z-score, α("alpha" at 5% significance level), and P-Value (probability value) in tabular form in rejecting the null hypothesis and accepting the alternative hypothesis as the true hypothesis stated in chapter one of this research. Thus consider the following Table.

Table 5.1.2: Test of Variables and Hypothesis

Variables	Z-score	P-value	α @ 5%
**RG	2.71	0.0034	0.05
**LRF	1.81	0.0351	0,05
**PSPG	1.83	0.0336	0.05
FES	-0.29	0.3859	0.05
**MC	2.28	0.0113	0.05
**DRS	2.11	0.0174	0.05
**CMR	1.98	0.0239	0.05
**MLDR	-2.51	0.0060	0.05
**Q/C	2.36	0.0091	0.05
TF	-1.56	0.0594	0.05
ICT	0.00	0.5000	0.05
**ERMP	-3.37	0.0011	0.05
**GGAT	2.01	0.0222	0.05
MoFEDR/A&NA	0.28	0.3897	0.05

(Source: SPSS 16.0 version and standard normal distribution statistical Table.)

Assuming that sound records keeping enhances good governance, accountability and transparency at MoFED institution, thus, the law of hypothesis states that:

a) Null hypothesis H_O: $\mu = 0$, that is, sound records keeping does not enhance good governance, accountability and transparency; and
b) Alternative hypothesis H_A: $\mu \neq 0$, that is, sound records keeping does enhance good governance, accountability and transparency. Assuming that μ is the population mean which is not equal to zero and often represented by the sample mean.

Note that GGAT is the dependent variable while the other variables are independent variables which are tested to prove the hypothesis at five percent (5%) significance level. It is statistically significant that controlling the independent variables will lead to a positive increase of the dependent variable based on the data collected. This research considered P-value as the significance probability of the observed value. Thus, if the calculated P-value is less than or equal to the stipulated level of significance of α, then H_O is rejected and H_A is accepted. On the other hand, if the calculated P-value is greater than the stipulated α, then H_O is not rejected but H_A is rejected. In statistical notation, $p \leq 0.05$ and the smaller this value the more confident H_O is rejected. Note also that any variable in the Table above, with double asterisks (**) is said to be statistically significant at 5% when H_O is rejected and H_A, which is the research hypothesis stated in chapter one of this research is accepted, and thus considers the hypothesis correct. Consequently, seventy-one percent(71%) of the variables tested as indicated in the probability value above are below five percent(5%) stipulated significance probability value of (α), which portrayed clearly that the hypothesis stated in chapter one of this research is correct.

In conclusion, the forgoing analysis portrays that there is evidence of records management development at MoFED with special reference to MoFED registry/administration. However, after 2005 strategies were being put to improve records management in Sierra Leone. It has made a giant strive in this drive. The establishment of records management development programme in any organisation ensures that records are systematically and efficiently created, captured, and described, secured, stored and preserved for long in the organisation in question and then transferred to archival institutions for national development. Thus, an average number of twenty-six (26) participants stated that MoFED registry/administration and the National Archives' vision and mission are of the developmental purposes in Sierra Leone. As records have unlimited enduring value, many of them remain accessible over time. Some of the records are demanded to continue very important government operations, document programmes, donor support, and others to provide legal evidence. However, records management and archival administration over the years in different countries have become a discipline which many people are now interested in studying so that the problems of management can be resolved. Thus, Sierra Leone is part of this massive development as there is a unit that offers Records Management and Archival Administration in the University of Sierra Leone, which the researcher thought that MoFED could send their staff for further training in order to minimise cost in managing vital records.

PART 6:
SUMMARY, CONCLUSIONS AND OBSERVATIONS

1. INTRODUCTION

This chapter focuses on the summary of findings, conclusions and observations of the study. The observations identified problems of records management at MoFED registry/administration in particular and MoFED in general which needs urgent solutions and implementation.

2. SUMMARY

The objectives of this study identify the types of records generated and received by MoFED; identify the records structures, procedures and regulatory requirements governing their keeping; investigate whether or not the management of records at MoFED is consistent with the life cycle concept of records keeping; investigate the staff training and competency in records keeping at MoFED; investigate the challenges staff and users face in managing and using records at MoFED; explore the relationship between the MoFED registry/administration and the National Archives among others.

This study employed questionnaire, interview, observation and documentary analysis as methods to collect data. The questionnaire to the MoFED registry/administration unit focus on: personal information; types of records generated/received; legal and regulatory framework; standard, codes, policies and procedures; facilities, equipment and supplies; monitoring and compliance with phases of records; disposition and retention procedures; users' security and training competencies; Information Communication Technology(ICT); good governance, transparency and accountability. In this study, both structured and unstructured questions were designed for each of these sub-scales. For ease of use and understanding, some items were adopted form Ellsberg and Heises' (2005) study. The draft questionnaire was pilot tested to ten (10) MoFED registry/administration staff, revised and categorised under ten (10) headings as indicated above. The first sub-scale sought information on staff such as name, staff category and designation followed by the third to the tenth sub-scales for which open and close questions were used; the three and five point Likert scales were used.

The main instruments were employed between the months of February and March 2018. Sixty (60) questionnaires were administered to collect data of which fifty 50(83.3%) were returned in usable form. Ten 10(16.7%) were not returned from the aforementioned category of staff to complement the study in question.

Data were analysed using Statistical Package for the Social Sciences (SPSS, Version 16) to compute frequencies, percentages and extrapolate pie and bar charts. SPSS was also used to compute Z-score and Probability value to test varied variables, which fourteen variables were tested as against the stipulated probability level of significance at five percent (5%).

The findings were revealing. On types of records generated, correspondences are mostly generated/received and there is a decentralised management of records practice at MoFED in general but MoFED registry/administration in particular is devoid of holding financial records. The findings also revealed that MoFED has laws and policies for the management of records but these policies are neither enforced nor effectively utilized to solve records management problems. The findings further revealed that there is inadequate trained and qualified middle level staff for managing records. Another finding was inadequate facilities, equipment and supplies at MoFED registry/administration to preserve records. The findings, further revealed that electronic records management exists but there are no formal electronic management policies especially with retention and disposition procedures; and there is a relationship between MoFED and the National Archives but not quite strong.

For the test of hypothesis of this research, it was revealed statistically that out of fourteen(14) variables tested, ten(10)(that is seventy-one percent (71%))of the variables qualified the test to reject the null hypothesis and accept the alternative hypothesis, which is the research hypothesis stated in chapter one. Those variables that did not pass the test statistically could be due to some errors committed during the research process or statistical computation. In this vein, it can be justifiable that all variables that passed this test, when well controlled in such a way could enhance good governance, accountability and transparency. Thus, this clearly signifies that records management practice is undergoing currently at MoFED.

3. CONCLUSIONS

In respect of the types of records generated/received, most were correspondences as portrayed with a percentage of sixty(60%), followed by public debt bulletins; grant application administration documents and progress reports. On the contrary, financial records should be managed in such a way that could enhance transparency by stakeholders who include Accountants and Records Managers. It is furthered that a well-qualified Accountant and Records Managers should be employed to manage financial records. It was also discovered that subject files, departmental files mainly comprising personnel files, and ministerial files are received/generated by them. The rationale was that the management of records at MoFED is based on decentralisation. Also those financial records are considered vital and should not be duplicated in order to avoid wastage of scarce resources. It was also revealed that the management of records at MoFED as a whole is cost-effective meaning that records are prudently managed. On this note, the cost-effectiveness of records management is all about managing the availability of allocated funds or resources of an organisation such as done in Ghana during the reform process. This is contrary to MoFED in general.

With regards legal and regulatory framework of the management of records, fifty-two percent (52%) participants agreed that there is Public Records/National Archives Act(1965) as primary legislation that provides direct guidance on the management of financial and non-financial records at MoFED. It was discovered that there exist other secondary legislation that serve as indirect guidance for the management of financial/non-financial records such as the 1991 National Constitution

Act, Right to Access Information (RAI) Act, 2013, and Finance and Audit Act, 2005. However, majority of the participants agreed that they are aware of such laws but not effectively and efficiently utilized; that these laws are not consistent with their requirements for managing records; and are not frequently up-dated due to their importance. It was also discovered that these laws mandate users to appraise, retain and dispose of public records. However, according to participants, these laws are seldom practised and enforced in Sierra Leone. Against this background, the archives and records management are based on records life cycle and appraisal. In this case even legally enforceable right of access to information is meaningless if government records are not in proper order. Even though many participants regarded records as a valuable commodity which could give huge benefits and merits, many organisations still do not take appropriate measures as the need is not pressing and no penalty levied for deliberate destruction of records. On this note, it is good that the Public Records Act, 1965 should be amended to suit the management of records in Sierra Leone, failing which the situation will be precarious.

On policies, standards, procedures and guidelines for managing records at MoFED registry/administration, it was discovered that forty-four percent(44%) agreed that there is adequate provision of written policies, standards, procedures for preparing and issuing retention schedules for the management of the Ministries' financial/non-financial and archives institutions but not effectively and efficiently utilized. On this note, the existence of policies serve as guidelines to facilitate actions and decisions to be taken. It is noted that advances in Information and Communication Technology (ICT) gives the opportunity for government to provide the delivery of information and services to citizens, and customers in order to enhance good governance. This is in agreement with the view that many organisations had policies before the institution of the reform programme but were informal and oral in order to manage their records effectively and efficiently. On this note, it is a fact that records policies are high level statements that offer overall direction (that is critical to the effectiveness of any records management project). These policies are said to be enshrined in the "Government Budgeting and Accountability Act, 2005" for the management of MoFED's financial records specifically and are admissible in the Court of Law to prove evidence of transparency and accountability. The findings also revealed that some of the procedures/instructions that provide guidance on the management of financial/non-financial records for example, Financial Instruction, Accountability Manual and Records Management Guidelines are not utilized because MoFED registry/administration did not hold or generate the Ministry's financial records. In other departments such as Accountant General Department(ADG) and Human Resource Management Office(HRMO) there were some restrictions on access and use of records. In this light, MoFED in general makes some efficient utilisation of financial records policies in order to achieve its mandate enshrined in the GBA Acts, 2005 and National Archives Act, 1965.

On the provision of facilities, equipment and supplies, the findings revealed that fifty-eight percent(58%) of the equipment(vertical file cabinets) is in the MoFED registry/administration for preserving/managing records; followed by lateral cabinet and guide/folders(supplies) respectively. The findings also noted that there is a budget allocation but not very sufficient to maintain storage equipment provided at MoFED registry/administration for the management of records. It was discovered that MoFED registry/administration does not have all the facilities, equipment and supplies such as public announcement system, shredder, computer diskette, shelves, and index cards and that all those in their possession are not sufficiently provided. In this vein, some of the listed furniture, office equipment and supplies that can be used for improving records management operations which include: library carts, telephone, public announcement system, and desk lamps. Further, it was discovered that storage facilities such as fire proof, safe, temperature control are not suitable. Thus, a good number of participants revealed that both financial/vital and non-financial records are not protected against disaster and that, there is no comprehensive documented disaster plan to protect MoFEDs strategic financial and records management system. In agreement with the aforementioned facilities, equipment and supplies an organisation should have a vital records protection programme as it will protect against those disasters and lessen the damage of facilities, equipment and supplies, but disaster will still happen and the result can be catastrophic to an organisation unless it has implemented policies and procedures gearing towards the protection of facilities, equipment and supplies.

On monitoring and compliance, it was revealed that MoFED registry/administration senior officials did monitor the management of records with respect to compliance of the phases of records keeping. Fifty-four percent (54%) participants agreed that these officials have keen interest in records management. This is manifested in the initial visit the researcher made to MoFED. He discovered that most of the records were organised and labelled both numerically and alphabetically which made the researcher subscribe to the view that senior officials did not only have interest but monitor the management of records. It was also discovered that MoFED registry/administration has a records centre headed by a records officer with records clerks. Further, participants who agreed that their officials do take active interest in the management of records also confirmed that they manage records in accordance with the three phases of records keeping. They defined active records as those generated and frequently used to carry out the day-to-day activities of MoFED administration; whereas semi-active records are not frequently used; inactive records are those that are no longer needed to carry out official duties and are transferred to the National Archives or offline and can be used for research purposes. These records are monitored by Records Managers, Archivists, Auditor Generals, Accountant General and Financial Secretary to ensure compliance with the three phases of records keeping. This practise at MoFED confirmed that the programme for managing financial records should be monitored on a regular basis. This should include systematic inspection of records managed by financial services in line ministries to ensure compliance with records management procedures and policies, identifying areas of strengths and weaknesses and measuring performance. Against this background it is contended that the monitoring systems in Sierra Leone concerning the management of records are inadequate and information is difficult to access.

For disposition and retention procedures, the findings were that fifty-two percent (52%) participants indicated that MoFED does retain records and dispose of some that are no longer useful. And that MoFED registry/administration does play an active role in the disposition and retention procedures. It was discovered that a retention period varied considerably from one unit to another within the Ministry. Some of the stated periods were: 1-6 years for financial records; 3 years, 5 years, 7 years, 10 years and 25 years for non-financial records. Although, some participants revealed that they retain records for long and others stated they have no specific time, a significant majority of participants in the registry/administration stated that the duration of retention period is seven (7) years. It is argued that non-financial and financial records are managed in the same way but the only difference is that some financial records have shorter lives than others. They furthered that both financial and non-financial records can be appraised; have a retention period ranging from 1-25 years; and can be archived for future use. However, retention period for financial records is 1, 2 and 6 years respectively On this note, records are kept in folders marked and placed in lateral cabinets or stored in hard and soft copies. Some of these records include ministerial files, departmental files and agencies files requesting for grant approval. For example, correspondences from the Office of the President files, Ministry of Agriculture and Food Security files, Ministry of Education, Science and Technology files, and public debt bulletins are all stacked in cabinets because information contained therein is of enduring value. Other records such as civil service personnel records are stacked in glass cabinets until the retirement age of sixty years is attained before they are qualified for archives. It was also discovered that at MoFED registry/administration, a significant majority of participants indicated that they preserved more of manual than electronic records. In manual formats records are received, sorted out, labelled and stacked in cabinets. Others revealed that records are kept in a cool (air conditioning), secure and dry place. For manual records hard copies are filed in big lever-arch files and kept in both metal and glass cabinets. Electronic records are kept on network servers in the ICT Unit and some other Units. Similarly, images of pdf are kept on back-up drives and savers. Electronic mail correspondences are kept on storage by Internet service providers in the ICT Unit. In this light, a survey report on Ho Polytechnique, a tertiary institution in Ghana, observed that the institution's records management is shifting from manual to electronic system by using computers and Internet facilities. Thus, electronic filing system prevents users from making serious mistakes that could affect the operations and image of the institution which is similar to MoFED.

With regards the users of records, security and training qualifications/competencies, participants indicated that users of MoFED's records are Ministers; the President; Financial Secretary; Development Secretary; Contract Officers/Local Technical Assistants(LTAs); Internal and External Auditors, Civil Servants, Records Practitioners, Researchers and the public. It is clear that MoFED registry/administration makes use of the Right to Access Information(RAI) Act, 2013 as it allows the general public to request for government records or information for the conduct of their business activities. In this regard, It is observed that records management programme intends to manage the life cycle of records effectively to ensure that records are known and available to the entire agency's staff that need to use them as supportive operation. It was also discovered that eighty percent(80%) of participants indicated that there are some challenges facing users/staff in the management of records which include inadequate trained and qualified records personnel at middle level, inadequate materials such as file covers, insufficient finance, inadequate space, insufficient logistical support, and slow Internet operations. However, modalities are put in place to salvage the situation, but the major challenge being funding and inadequate trained and qualified staff. On this note, a study found that management population services in Kenya faced a plethora of challenges, the major being, lack of policies, standard procedures and guidelines to enhance the effective and efficient management of financial records. The study included other issues such as low priority accorded to records management, absence of records management culture, and inadequate skills for managing both manual and electronic record formats. These are similar to the management of records by MoFED registry/administration and MoFED in general.

The findings also revealed that fifty-eight percent(58%) of participants indicated that records are not always missing, misplaced, lost or damaged files at MoFED registry/administration. In essence, it was interesting to note that only six percent (6%) of participants stated that records seldom got lost, missing, misplaced or damaged. On the contrary, there were cases of missing, misplaced, loss or damaged records at Sierra Leone public sector organisations including MoFED registry/administration.

On qualifications, it was discovered that seventy-four percent(74%) participants, indicated that MoFED registry/administration staff have qualifications/competencies in the management of records but are not sufficient to manage records effectively and efficiently to achieving the Ministry's ultimate goal. In this case, most staff have higher educational qualifications with basic records management training at least to manage the MoFED registry/administration records. Staff, including records officers and their clerks, are all capacitated with basic computer skills in the management of MoFED records. And competence could make possible to identify required educational standards, training needs, level of experience and, whenever possible, practical expertise required by staff responsible for managing financial records. Where there is a relevant scheme of service in place of records staff, job specification must incorporate the qualifications specified by the scheme.

For training facilities forty-eight percent(48%) participants indicated that there are no training facilities for staff at MoFED registry/administration for the management of records. However, twenty percent (20%) participants did agree that there are some records management training activities given to new staff during their induction exercise. On this note, the induction training should be provided in a timely fashion to all civil servants. Records staff should receive detailed guidance in their induction training to help them understand the structure and duties for the management of records. It is evident that MoFED does undertake internal training programmes on the life cycle of records; guidance for records management performance for the proper management of financial and non-financial records during the induction training exercise. However, in the closed interview conducted with some staff at the Accountant General Department(AGD), there are some aspects of the life cycle of records management training for all categories of staff. The reason being, they manage records that are sensitive in nature and thus should not be held by any unit in order to prevent duplicity. This is consistent with the researcher's view as MoFED registry/administration is the epicentre for all administrative affairs and should also manage financial records. Thus in Sierra Leone, there are still problems of training facilities for records staff.

On Information Communication and Technology(ICT), the findings revealed that a hundred percent(100%) indicates that there is an ICTs unit at MoFED providing ICTs and related services to departments/units. This is evidenced in the provision of a special ICTs unit that oversees the operation of computer devices and ensures the proper maintenance of both hardware and software systems at the Ministry. It also provides training facilities to staff. The system's performance is always checked and virus protection often provided. It was also discovered that the ICTs unit provides Internet facilities to all units within MoFED in order to strengthen Information and Communication Technology (ICT) amongst staff and the public at large to access certain records for national development. On this note there are types of electronic records such as e-mail, voicemail, Geographic Information System (GIS). Web-page, work process document, spreadsheet, database, digital image, video and audio files. In essence, most MoFED records concerning developmental activities are online and offline. Thus, the majority of participants indicated that MoFED records, especially finance records, are allowed in courts of law as evidence to testify against quilt. On this note, there are two main areas of data protection requirements apart from the general one: the ability of electronic records to satisfy legal requirements and the admissibility of records as evidence in a court of law.

With regards electronic records management policies, it was revealed that seventy-two percent(72%) of participants did not know whether or not there is a formal electronic management policy. It was discovered that MoFED practised electronic records systems without any written policy in place and merely base its records management on their instinct and initiative, far from complying with international standards of best practice. Against this background, the existence of policies serve as guidelines to facilitate actions and decisions to be taken. It is noted that advances in Information and Communication Technology (ICT) provide the opportunity for government to improve the delivery of information and services to citizens and businesses to streamline public sector functions, and increase public participation in governance. It was discovered that MoFED has a system of computer transaction records keeping being always transferred to Archives or offline for research purpose on pdf, free encyclopaedia; and computer transactions have never been deleted from the system without disposition instructions. On this note, the "White Paper of KSHS" maintained that electronic records keeping under the responsibility of agencies should ensure that electronic records keeping policies and procedures are developed and implemented as part of overall plans. This is not contrary to MoFED registry/administration as many participants indicated that it is not to their knowledge that a written electronic management policy exists.

On good governance, transparency and accountability, the findings were that eighty-six percent(86%) indicated that sound records keeping enhances good governance, accountability and transparency in varied ways such as managing government funds; keeping proper records can increase Gross Domestic Product(GDP) and ensure equitable distribution of national resources; taking immediate and accurate decisions; promoting prudent financial management through tackling fraud and promoting climate of trust; discourage mismanagement of consolidated funds and ensure equitable distribution of these funds to varied MDAs;

enhance quick and sound decision making and expedient retrieval of information for developmental purposes; and consistently help achieve efficiency, effectiveness and productivity in MoFED. This finding is consistent with the view that advocating for good governance should be part of a records and archives management profession. It is only when certain principles are applied to the process of financial records identification which could be easily retrieved for decision making in public sector financial institutions, that the concept of good governance and accountability is meaningful, which MoFED is no exception. The findings further revealed that there is a culture of records keeping and top management support records keeping. If there was contrary, it will affect the functioning of government activities thereby deterring accountability, transparency and good governance system. Also, it is maintained that some of the pillars of good governance and democracy was transparency, probity and accountability, which can be achieved through proper records management systems. However, it is further noted that the breakdown of financial system is often related to breakdown in records management. In this case, records management reinforces financial control and support accountability and transparency. Thus, at MoFED, these findings revealed that proper management of both financial and non-financial records were the basis for supporting economic development and provide good governance, accountability, and transparency. These are the fundamental variables that propel democracy, improve financial service delivery and reduce poverty.

With regards the relationship between MoFED registry/administration and National Archives, it was revealed that there is a relationship between them. These are the corporate memories of the Ministry that have research value as stated by fifty-two percent (52%) participants. It is contended that archives are apolitical, and cannot be seen only as preserving records for historical research or warehouse for old records no longer in current administrative use. And records management, on the other hand, embarks on the management of both private and public entities records for efficiency, competitive advantage, and strategic value, increase of profit and avoidance of loss. The findings also revealed that the National Archivists, Records Managers in the public sector, and MoFED work in tandem to achieve national development. The findings revealed that the Archivists and Records Managers contribute to the drafting of an amended National Archives Act, which contains among others the retention, disposition, and access authorisation policies. On this premise it is only archival institutions that do external monitoring across governments according to agreed inspection plans. This mandate can be extended to the drafting of a records retention policy that can be included in the national constitution as done in countries such as South Africa, Ghana, and Kenya. Thus, this finding revealed that there is official relationship between MoFED registry/administration and the National Archives as the latter are a statutory body responsible for handling government records across the board. Some of those records transferred to the National Archives are department files, ministerial files, and even some personnel files after being qualified for archives. For example a significant number of participants stated seven(7) years as the retention period after which they can be transferred to the National Archives. The same goes for personnel records. After the retirement age of staff, all records concerning such staff are sent to the National Archives seven (7) years from their retirement age.

4. OBSERVATIONS

This study discovered that financial records are not held in MoFED registry/administration as per mandate and responsibilities; it is supposed to hold all types of records. This unit is the epicentre of the Ministry which cuts across all units and thus should hold financial records in order to enhance transparency in the management of records. It is necessary for the centralisation of records to exist side-by-side with the decentralisation system at MoFED so as to enhance proper management of records. The researcher believed that for any records created by the varied units at MoFED, the copy should be sent to MoFED administration in order to enhance transparency and accountability especially financial records.

MoFED utilises both primary and secondary legislations to dispense the management of records, but these laws are not consistent with their requirement and frequently reviewed. It was also discovered that the laws are not enforced by levying penalties such as paying (of huge sums of money) or put behind bars by anyone who deliberately loss or misplace records. Thus, it is good that these laws are made consistent, regularly reviewed with heavy penalties levied on defaulters. The researcher believed that if Public Records Act, 1965 is updated, it will bring a huge benefit in the management of records to all public sector organisations in Sierra Leone and MoFED is no exception.

MoFED has written policies, standard, procedures and instructions to manage the life cycle of records but are not effectively and efficiently utilised. Thus, stringent measures should be taken to achieve the ultimate goal of the Ministry. The researcher is of the move that the rationale for effective and efficient utilisation of records management policies will enhance sound records keeping and minimise the loss /damage of records.

The findings revealed that there are not enough facilities, equipment and supplies at MoFED registry/administration as compared to other units within the Ministry. And it was discovered that the Ministry does not have any comprehensive disaster management plan in other to protect these facilities, equipment and supplies. It is justifiable that the MoFED registry/administration is provided with more advanced equipment backed by a comprehensive disaster management plan as in Ghana and Malaysia to avoid unexpected costs. The researcher subscribed to this fact that if more sophisticated facilities and equipment are supplied at MoFED administration, it will discourage the habit of depositing records on the floor and the records will be protected from insects, rodents etc.

It was discovered that the monitoring of records at the Ministry is only limited to financial records at the Accountant General Department (AGD). It is advised that monitoring of records be done for all sorts of records generated/received at MoFED. The reason for this is to minimise corruption at the Ministry. As corruption hinders development.

It is also advisable that MoFED employs additional trained and qualified middle level staff for the management of both paper and electronic records. At MoFED registry/administration there is no written policy on the management of electronic records such as users logging in and out; staff not allowed to disclose information e.g payroll; staff not allowed to do private work within the departments; users being staff and having usernames and passwords; and all documents submitted to the ICT Manager for back-up and proper recording. There is a demand for a development of a written policy on electronic records management. The rationale for this development is to avoid unauthorised access to valuable records such as payroll, and some other financial records by unauthorised users.

Further there should be a strong collaboration between the National Archives and MoFED registry/administration in particular and MoFED in general. This could be in the form of signing a Memorandum of Understanding(MoU) between them; the organisation of sensitisation workshops on good records practice; and spearheading training facilities for civil servant records practitioners. Increased publicity of records management could help raise awareness for the government and citizens especially with regards the role of records practitioners in promoting accountability, and transparency. These techniques should be applied because both administrative and archival records are pivotal for the socio-economic development of Sierra Leone. In fact in countries such as South Africa and England it is the Archivist that solely is responsible for the recruiting and training of records practitioners, which signifies a good relationship. Thus MoFED should follow such activities.

There should be provision for further research on records management at MoFED for improved performance and the promotion of good governance, accountability and transparency. The reason being research on the management of records at public sector organisation is very limited, besides any organisation that does not embark on frequent research on its management of records will hardly develop or achieve it ultimate goal. This will provide opportunity for acquiring new techniques for records management performance at MoFED in particular.

BIBLIOGRAPHY

Abbott, Brad (2006). *The Electronic Communication and Transaction Act 2000: Its implications to record keeping in South Africa.* Available at https://www.national archive-gov.za/site/default/file/managing-records-policy-principles-and- requirement April-2006.pdf. Accessed on 10/4/2017.

ACARM(2007). *Records Management Guide.* London: University Press Akotia, Pino(2008). "Consequences of a failure to manage public financial records," *ESARBICA Journal, 24(3), 2-16.*

Akotia, Pino(2012). *Records management principles and practice.* Legon: NAB superior Service. Available at http//www.ajo.info/index.php/esarjo/article/view/30958 Accessed on 20/5/2017.

Akotia, Pino and Adjei, Emmanual(2004)."Governance and the management of public sector financial records,"*GIMPA Journal of Leadership, Management and Administration,* 2(1), 30-36.

Akussah, Harry(2015). "The challenges of Managing Electronic Records in Developing Countries: Implication for Records Managers in Sub-Sahara African," *Records Management Journal,* 25(2), 153-196.

Akussah, Harry and Asamoah, C (2015). "Management of public sector records in Ghana: a descriptive survey,". *Records Management Journal,* 25(2), 183-196.

Available at http://doi.org/10.1108/RMJ-10-2014-0044. Accessed on 9/10/2017.

Argyriades, D.(2002). *Governance and Public Administration in the 21st Century: New Trend and New Techniques.* Brussels: International Institute of Administrative Services. Available at https://books.google.com.sl/books?id=cD=caz0GRy4C&pg=PA180&dq=governance+administration+in+the+21st+century:+New+trend+and+New+Tech. Accessed on 12/10/2017.

Asamoah, Catherine (2015)."The Benefit of Electronic Records Management Systems: A General Review of Published and Some Unpublished Cases," *Records Management Journal*, 25(2), 196-209.

Bantin, P (2007)."The Indiana University Electronic Record Project: Analysing Function, Identifying Transactions and Evaluating Recordkeeping System. A Report on Methodology, Archives and Museum Information," *A Cultural Heritage Informatics Quarterly*, 10, 246-66

Bohn, J (2002). "Corporate Governance: a new risk element in corporate finance." Available at https// www.cipe.org/publication/fs/index.hm . Accessed 30/01/2017.

Bunn, Jenny (2009). "From polders to postmodernism: a concise history of archival Theory," *Records Management Journal*, 19(3), 253-254. Available at https:/doi.org/10.1108/89565690910999265. Accessed on 10/10/2017.

Burke, Alex (2015). "About records management eHow Contributor," *From Free Encyclopedia*. Accessed on 10/10/2017.
Carter, R.G.S.(2006). "Of things and unsaid: power, archival silences, power in silence," *Archivaria,* 61,215-233. Available at https://www.researchgate.net/publication/290228653-07-things-said-and-unsaid-power-archival-silence-and-power-in-silence. Accessed on 12/6/2017.

Creswell, J.W (2009). *Research Design: Qualitative, Quantitative and Mixed Methods Approach.* Thousand Oaks, CA: Sage Publication.

Collins, M. (2009). *The foundations of social research*. London: Sage Publication. Available at http:www.worldcat.org/title/foundation_of_social_research…and_research…/39076972. Accessed on 10/01/2018.

David, Rodreck(2017). "Contribution of records management to audit opinions and accountability in governance," Available at http:www. doi:10.10.4102/sajim.v19/1.771. Accessed from pdf. on16/09/2017.

DeMarrias, K.(2004). Qualitative interview studies: Learning through experience. K.

DeMarrias and S.D. Lapan(eds). Foundations for research (pp.51-68). Mahwah, N J: erlbaum. Available at http://www.researchgate.net/…/2914564_qualitative_interview_through_Experience. Accessed on 13/01/2018.

Digital Government Institute (2017). "Records management conference and expo," Washington DC: Walter E. Washington Convention Centre. Available at https://10times.com/records-management-conference-expo. Accessed on 9/10/17.

Ellsberg, M and Heise, Lori(2005). *Researching violence against women: a practical guide for researchers and activists*. Geneva: World Health Organisation.

Faulhaber, Patricia(2015)."The definition of records management eHow Contributor*," Free Encyclopedia*. image:www.office.micorsoft.com. Accessed on 21/10/2017.

Financial Management System &Guidelines (2015).*Records keeping: what to keep, and for how long and how the human resource managing financial records are controlled?* Available at http://bizcconnect.standardbank.co.za/manage/human resource/financial management…/record-keeping. Accessed on 4/10/2017.

Free Encyclopedia(2004). *Policy on retention of financial records.* Available at w.Saga.org.Za/.../FPG%2009520Retention%200f%20Financial/RM%20 Policy%20management2.pdf/. Accessed on 8/09/2017.

Free Encyclopedia(2018). *Standard score.* Available at http://wikipedia.org/wiki/standard_score. Accessed on 18/05/2018.

Government of Sierra Leone. *Government Budgeting and Accountability Act 2005* (2005). Freetown: Government Printing Department(Unpublished). *Constitution of Sierra Leone 1991*(1991). Freetown: Government Printing Press (Unpublished).

Gregory, K. (2005). "Implementing an electronic records management system: a public sector case study," *Records Management Journal*, 15(2), 80-85.

IRMT (2009).*Electronic information for accountability workshops sourcebook. International Bank for Reconstruction and Development.* London:

World Bank. (2002). *Electronic records management: concepts and issue.* London:

IRMT. (2006). National Records Centre for Sierra Leone: training guide series. London:

IRMT. (2007).*Electronic government, corruption and records management charting the way forward, a training guideline.* London:

IRMT. (2011). *Principle and practice of financial records management.* imrt.org/document/assessment tool/msfr.pdf. Accessed on 7/10/2017.

I S O 15489:2001 Standards. "*Records Management.*" Available at http:en.wikipedia.org/wiki/Records-Management. Accessed on 23/4/2017.

Jalloh, Mohamed(2017). *An assessment of MoFED's records in enhancing good governance in Sierra Leone.* [interview] 24th April.

Kansas Records Management Guidelines.(2012). Available at http://www.kshs.org/government/records/electronic/electronicrecordsguidlines.htm Accessed on 23/4/2017.

Kansas State Historical Society (2007)."*Kansas electronic records keeping strategy: a white paper.*" File:// F:/Kansas%20Electronic%20Records%20manage

Kargbo, John A (2009). "The connection between good governance and record keeping: the Sierra Leone experience,'' *Journal of Society of Archivists*, 30(2), 249-260 (2015). "Primary records: what future?,*"* *Library Review,* 65(1/2), 84-92. Available at http://www.emeraldinsights.com/doi/10.1108/LR-08.2015-0082. Accessed on 18/11/2017. (2005)"Archives management in post war Sierra Leone: luxury or necessity?,"*Journal of the Society of Archivists*, 26(2), 243-250

Kelusopr, T.W and Ngulube, P (2012). "Records management practice in Labour Organisation in Botswana," *South Africa Journal of Information,* Available at dx.doi.org/10.4102/sajim.v14i/-513. Accessed on 19/10/2017.

Lansana, Abdul Raheem (2017). *An assessment of MoFED's records in enhancing good governance* [Interview]. 6th July. (Unpublished)

Malemelo, Fadzai, AdockDube, Rodreck, N.D and Patrick Ngulube(2013). "Management of financial records at Marondera Municipality in Zimbabwe,"*Journal of South Africa Society of*

Archivists, 64(1). Available at file:///E://Management%20of%20financialrecords%20at%20th%20Marondera%20. Accessed on 20/9/2017.

Mason, J(2002). *Qualitative research* 3rd ed. Thousand oaks, Ca: Sage Publications. Available at http://www.swt.uevora.pt/wp-content/uploads/2013/03/mason.2002.pdf. Accessed on 16/01/2018.

McChure, C and Sprehe, T.J(2008). *Guideline for electronic records management on state and federal agencies websites.* London: Information

Management Association, Inc. Available at http://www.cni.org/wp-content/upload/2013/06/Guidelines-for-Electronic-Records management-on.pdf. Accessed on 15/5/2017.

McDonald, J(2005). "The wild frontier ten years on," McLeod, J and Hare, S. Managing Electronic Records. *A Journal of Interdisciplinary Research,* 1(1), 28- 67.

Mclean, Robert(2003). "The business case for implementing ISO 15489." *Records Management Bulletin,* Issue 115, 7-12.

McLeod, Julie (2007). *Managing Records: Electronic Records.* New York: State Archives. Available at http:/www.emeraldinsights.com/doi/10.1108/0956907.0833116. Accessed on 24/7/2017.

Memorial University of Newfoundland (2008).*Record Management.* Ottawa: Newfoundland and Labrador.

Merriam, S.B.(2009). *Qualitative research: a guide to design and implementation.* San Francisco: Joesey-Bass. Available at http://books.google.com.sl/books/about/Qualitative_Research.html.pid=tvFLcrgcuSlC_&redir_esc=y. Accessed on 13/01/2018.

Moore, Albert(2015).*Sierra Leone News: EBOLA FALL OUT: Re: Financial management and records keeping in Sierra Leone.* File///F:/sierra Leone News EBOLA FALL OUT Re Financial management accessed from pdf on 16th/9/2017.

Mokhtar, Asma Umi and Yusof, Z.M(2009). "Electronic records management in the Malaysian public sector: the existence of policy," *Records Management Journal*, 19(3), 231-244. Available at http://doi.org/0.1108/09565690910999201. Accessed on 6/10/2017.

Montana, John (2008)."Electronic records management in a small office," *GPSOLO Magazine.* Available at http://www.americanbar.org/newsletter/publication/gp_solo_ma. Accessed on 20/9/2017.

Musembi, Masila (2005).*Efficient records management as a basis of Good governance*. Nairobi: National Archive and Documentation Services.

Myburg, Sue (2005). ''Record management and archives: finding common ground,"*The Information Management Journal,* 6(4), 24-29. Available at https://pdf.semanticscholar.org/bafb/f7b21da07f08a446684d1e5839a1e.pdf. Accessed on 20/10/2017.

National Archives of Scotland (2003).*Records Policies- the National Archives of Scotland.* Available at http://www.nas.gov.uk/recordskeeping/records Policies. Asp. Accessed on 19/04/ 2017.

National Archives and Records Service (2006). The state of electronic records management in South Africa. Available at http://www.nars.gov.uk/electronic recordkeeping/records policies. Accessed on 18/05/2017.

Nengomasha, C (2013). "The past, present and future of records and archives management in sub- Sahara Africa," *Journal of the South African Society of Archivists,* 46, 2-12. Available at https://www.ajol.info/index.php/jsasa/article/view/10084. Accessed on 7th/11/2017.

Neuman, L.W.(2011). *Social research method: qualitative and quantitative approach 6th ed.* Boston: Pearson. Available at http://www.pearson.com/us/higher- education/program/Nueman-social-Research-Metheis-Qualitative-and-Quantitative- Approach-7th-edition//RGM74573.html. Accessed on 16/01/2018.

New York State United Court System , Office of Records Management (2003). *Essential components of an efficient records storage facilities.* Available at http://www.nycorts.gov/admin/recordsmanagement/pubs_training/essential-comp- rec-storage.pdf. Accessed on 24th June, 2017.

Ngoepe, Mpho (2007).*Accountability, transparency and good governance: the National Archive and Record Service in South Africa's role in helping government to better service delivery to the South Africans.* Pretoria: South Africa press.

Okafor,T.G(2012). *Public sector financial management: a panacea for good governance.* Available at http://www.ajol.info/index.php/ijah/article/view/106364. Accessed on 7/11/2017.

Oyunga, Roman(2015). *Records management in a Non-Governmental Organisation (NGO).* A case study of Population Services International Kenya(PSK).Ur:http://hd/.handle.net/123456789/1220.File:///G:/Records%20manage mnt%20in%20Non-Government%20organisation. Accessed on 7/10/2017.

Parliamentary Monitoring Group (2016). *State of Archives & challenges in South Africa National Archivist briefing; strategies overview & future plans*. Available at http://pmg.org.Za/committee-meeting/22093/. Accessed on 29/9/2017.

PRISM(2016)."Why records management? "International Conference Paper. Webinar. Available at www.prismint/.org/Buy-From-a-PRISM-member/Free Resource/why-record-managements.html. Accessed on 3/02/2017.

Public Policy Forum(2013). "Record management." Milwaukee: Public Policy Forum. Available at https//www.publicpolicyforum.org. Accessed on 9/06/2017.

Republic of South Africa(2002). Electronic Communication and Transaction Act (Act.No.25 of 2002).

Richards, L. (2002). Handling Qualitative Data. London: Sage Publication. Available at http:amazon.co.uk/Handling-Data-Lyn-Richards/dp/1446276066. Accessed on 20th/01/2018.

Richie, J, Lewis J, and Elam, M. (2003).Designing and selecting sample. Richie and Lewis (Eds). *Qualitative research practice: A guide for social science students and Researchers*; (pp.77-108). London: Sage Publications. Available at http://mthayibi.files.wordpress.com/2011/10/qualitative_research_practice_a_guide_for_social_science_students_and_researchers_jane_ritchie_and_Lewis_eds_20031. pdf. Accessed on 22/01/2018.

Sadik, Alhassan A(2015)."Digital Records Keeping Workshop Held in Accra," *Records Management Journal*, 4, 56-58. Available at http://www.ghanaweb.com/GhanaHomePage/regional/digital-Recordkeeping- workshop-held-in-Accra-382458. Accessed on 20/4/2017.

Saffady, Williams(2004). *Records and Information Management Fundamentals of Professional Practice.* Leneda: ARMA International. Available at http://www.barnsandnoble.com/w/recors-and-information-management-william- saffady/110/718825. Accessed on 20/4/2017.

Salkind, Neil J (2006).*Exploring research.* 4th ed. New Jersey: Prentice Hull.

Salkind, N.J(2011). *Exploring Research.* 8th ed. New Jersey: Prentice Hall. Available at http://www.peyperearsonstore.com/bodutote/exploring_research_978020 5093816 Accessed on 11/01/2018.

Schneck, Thomas (2015).*7 mistake to avoid in financial records management.* Available at http://blog.docuware.com/document-management/7-mistake-to-avoid. Accessed on 7/10/2017.

Shepherd, Elizabeth(2015). "Implementing Electronic Management System: A Public Sector Case," *Records Management Journal, Aslib,* 1(4), 15-24. Available at http://intterparastrust.org/assets/dissenination/ACARMSymposiumjune2 015.pdf. Accessed on 10/09/2017. Sierra Leone Gazette No. 21, Wednessday 30th April, 2008.

Sierra Leone MoFED (2012). *Integrating public financial management reform project…in strengthening records management at Accountant General, Records Department.* Availabe at mofed.gov.sl/…100-integrated-public-financial- management-reform-project. Accessed on 12/09/2017.

Sierra Leone Ministry of Information and Communication(2016). *The country year book of Sierra Leone.* Freetown: Hamilton Wise Communication Ltd. *Ministry and Functional Review of the Ministry of*

Finance and Economic Development (MoFED). Freetown: Public Sector Reform Unity. From pdf. Accessed on January 15,2017.

State Archives and Records of New South Wales (2017). *Machine learning and records management.* Available at http://futureproof.records.nsw.gov.au. Accessed on 12/10/2017.

State Records of South Australia(2007*). Managing Electronic Records Issues.*

Statistics Sierra Leone (2016). *2015 population and housing census- summary of final result*. Freetown: Sierra Leone Press(Unpublished).

Tagbotor, D.P, R.N.Adzido and P.G. Agbanu (2015). "Analysis of records management and organisational performance," *International Journal of Academic Research in Accounting, Finance and Management Science*, 5(2), 1-16, Doi:10.6007/IJARAFMS/v5-i2/1557. Accessed on 9/10/2017.

Tafor, Vivian (2007). "Good Governance and records keeping: is there anything more we can do?,"*ESSRBICA Newsletter*,20(3),23-57.

Tale, Setareki and Alefaio, Opeta(2005). "Record Management in Developing Countries Challenges and Threats- Towards Realistic Plan," *ACARM Newsletter*, Issue 37, Winter. Available at http://www.fichier-pdf.fr/2011/03/18/37-6-records management-in-developing-countrirs-challenges-and-threats. Accessed on 4/3/2017.

Thurston, Anne(2002) *Management of Recorded Information*. London: IRMT.

Tough, Alistair(2006). "Records and transition to digital*,"* Tough, A and Moss, M (eds).*Records keeping in hybrid environment. Managing the creation, use, preservation and disposal of unpublished information objects in context*. Oxford: Chandos publishing, 1-25. (2009). "Leading and managing Archives and records programme strategies for success,"

Records Management Journal, 19(3), 252-253. Available at http://doi.org/10.1108/09565690910999256. Accessed on 9/10/2017.

Turay, Salieu (2017). *An assessment of the management of public sector records in enhancing good governance in the MoFED*[Interview]. 8th June. (Unpublished).

Venter, L(2007). "National Archives and records service requirements for the management of electronic records in the public sector: an archivist perspective on records management vs. storage management," *Archive News*, 2, 22-36. Available at http://www.journal.sageup.com/doi/abs/10.1177/0266666914550492. Accessed on 17/6/2017.

Wikipedia,FreeEncyclopedia (2003).*National Archives and Records Administration*. Available online at http;//en.wikipedia.org/wiki/National-Archives- and- Records-Administration.Accessed on 18/04/2017.

Williams, C. (2006). *Managing Archives: foundation, principle and practice*. Oxford: Chandos Publishing. Available at http://www..amazon.co.uk/managing-Archives- foundation-Infomation-professional/dp/1843341131.Accessed on 12/7/2017.

Word Bank Group Archives (2007).*Records keeping and accountability*. New York: World Bank.

Yusof, Z. Mohamed (2009). "Nurturing attitudes for records management in Malaysia financial institution," *Records Management Journal*, 19(3), 218-230, http:/doi/10.1108/09565690910999210. Accessed on 23/09/2017.

Zucker, Donna M.(2009). *Teaching research methods in the humanities and social sciences: how to do case study research*. Massachusetts: University of Massachusetts. Available at

. Accessed on 12/01/2018.

www.ingramcontent.com/pod-product-compliance
Lightning Source LLC
Chambersburg PA
CBHW071212160426
43196CB00011B/2264